LOST BRITAIN

LOST BRITAIN

David Long

Michael O'Mara Books Limited

LOST BRITAIN

David Long

Michael O'Mara Books Limited

A CIP catalogue record for this book is available from the British Library.

Papers used by Michael O'Mara Books Limited are natural, recyclable products made from wood grown in sustainable forests. The manufacturing processes conform to the environmental regulations of the country of origin.

ISBN: 978-1-78243-439-9 in hardback print format
ISBN: 978-1-78243-441-2 in e-book format

1 3 5 7 9 10 8 6 4 2

Jacket picture sources: Stocks and Pillories, Old Sarum and Local Time from Clipart.com

Designed and typeset by Design 23
Printed and bound by CPI Group (UK) Ltd, Croydon, CR0 4YY

www.mombooks.com

Contents

INTRODUCTION

Britain is a place steeped in history: it has several famous World Heritage Sites, dozens of designated battlefields and protected shipwrecks, thousands of conservation areas, tens of thousands of Scheduled Ancient Monuments and hundreds of thousands of historic, listed buildings – and these make up just a tiny fraction of our history. Yet, for a country that has preserved so much of its past, an awful lot has been lost.

Over the centuries, priceless treasures have disappeared, exceptional buildings have been torn down, potentially world-changing technologies quietly killed off and entire settlements wiped out by wars or a catastrophe of nature. Sometimes the search for them has never been called off – for example in the Fens where King John's crown jewels are thought to have vanished. But, more often, there is no hope of recovery because the loss has been total or because no one has any clear idea of where to look.

Sometimes all we have left are a few tantalizing clues in a fading document, an odd fragment of carved stone poking through the grass or a shadowy outline made visible only by the magic of ground-penetrating radar. But exploring history this way can be thrilling and more rewarding than traipsing along the heritage trail where all the romance has been lost to the coaches, queues and crowds. This book, I hope, provides the perfect place to begin your search.

DAVID LONG,
BRENT ELEIGH, SUFFOLK

Anne Boleyn's Heart

Suffolk

HENRY VIII WAS CONSIDERATE ENOUGH
to pay £23 for a French swordsman to behead
his wife – it's a cleaner cut than when using an
executioner's axe – but showed no such care when
it came to burying her remains.

While in itself not exactly surprising, the horribly casual disposal of the dead queen came to light in the 1870s during work on the chapel of St Peter ad Vincula in the Tower of London. Lifting the chancel floor, workmen found thousands of bones, including those of a young woman crammed unceremoniously into an old elm munitions box.

Forensic examination revealed that these were 'all perfectly consolidated and symmetrical and belong to the same person'. It was also apparent that the skull, with its 'large eyes, oval face, and rather square full chin', was in entirely the wrong place for someone who had been buried in one piece. There was no evidence of the rumoured sixth finger, but little doubt that it was the body of Anne Boleyn.

Sensitive to the status of these and other remains, which included another two queens, two saints and numerous noblemen, Queen Victoria determined they should be reburied in a more respectful and orderly fashion. What would not have been apparent at this time, however, was that Anne may well have been missing something other than just her head.

At such a distance and with her death surrounded by

myth, the truth is impossible to verify, but for centuries many have believed that the queen's heart was removed after her execution and then spirited away from the capital.

Some say this was done on the orders of Henry, but it seems unlikely that he would trouble to give this order, only then to show no interest at all in what happened to the rest of her. Others insist it was her uncle who rescued the organ, Sir Philip Parker of Erwarton Hall in Suffolk, returning home with it and arranging for an interment in the local parish church dedicated to St Mary.

It is a colourful story, typical of the kind of romantic drama that is attributed to doomed royals. The difference with this tale is that it might have some substance. The decoration on the font in St Mary's church includes a rather singular Tudor rose, and the local pub is called the Queen's Head. The clincher, however, is the discovery of a small heart-shaped lead casket in 1837. By then it contained nothing more substantial than dust, but this and the suggestion it was reburied beneath the organ has proved to be more than enough to keep the legend alive.

Back-to-Backs

Birmingham

A VICTORIAN INNOVATION, BUILT AT A TIME OF rapid population expansion and increasing urbanization, the back-to-back house provided a cheap way of accommodating the poor, although its shortcomings very quickly became apparent.

In most British towns and cities, specific laws make it illegal to run a washing line across the street, but for decades working-class families in cities such as Birmingham, Leeds, Liverpool and Manchester had no choice. From the 1830s they were crammed into back-to-backs, dingy slum terraces in which pairs of terraced houses shared their back walls, leaving no room for even the meanest yard.

Sharing their side walls with the neighbours as well meant that such dwellings could be built very cheaply and quickly. Unfortunately, the resulting paucity of doors and windows meant the houses were poorly lit and ventilated. The inevitable overcrowding also meant that sanitation, such as it was, was arguably of an even lower standard than was normal for the times.

Various initiatives after the Great War, such as Homes for Heroes[1] and the 1919 Housing Act, eventually led to these back-to-backs being swept away. As part of a nationwide programme of slum clearance and council-house building, for the first time ever, local authorities were required by law to provide decent housing as a social necessity. Today, as a result, just a single block of original back-to-backs survive intact.

Carefully preserved by the National Trust, numbers 50–54 Inge Street and 55–63 Hurst Street in Birmingham offer an insight into the lives of the many hundreds of thousands of workers who were crammed into similar properties over the course of more than a century. One can only try to imagine the filth and squalor, because essential restoration work has left the old buildings looking rather nice. But by incorporating shop fronts as well as houses and workshops in a single block, this unique survivor gives a good impression of the crushingly claustrophobic and cheek-by-jowl nature of life and work for many ordinary Victorians.

---

1. Who now remembers that Peacehaven on the south coast was originally called New Anzac-on-Sea and was originally planned as a settlement for returning Australian ans New Zealand troops.

Barings Bank

City of London

ONCE A KINGPIN OF ENGLISH MERCHANT BANKING,
Barings' 1995 collapse made headlines around
the world, although in the light of subsequent
scandals its losses of just over £800 million seem
almost modest.

Britain has many old and venerable banks. As the queen's banker, Coutts & Co. enjoys a certain cachet, and C. Hoare is still run by the descendants of its founder after eleven generations and nearly 350 years. Barings was a comparative newcomer to the City of London, but was nevertheless counted among this same elite once upon a time.

Established in London in the 1760s, the bank's German partners rapidly assimilated into society and joined the British establishment. Gaining a couple of baronetcies together with several baronies and viscounties and two earldoms, Baring family members went on to become MPs, government ministers and Knights of the Garter while holding senior positions in both the military and diplomatic services.

For more than two centuries, the bank trundled along without trouble, very much the engine for the family's social advancement as well as the source of its wealth. In 1802 it played a leading role in the Louisiana Purchase – strictly speaking, the American government bought nearly 530 million acres from the bank, rather than from Napoleon – and a decade later, Barings provided much of the funding for the war of 1812. At other times it employed a more cautious approach, ceding its position to rivals such as Rothschild, a tactic that may have enabled the company to weather the Great Depression in 1929 better than many other British banks.

Barings had no such luck in the 1990s, however, when the activities of a single trader began to pile up substantial losses. Extraordinarily, the bank's own system enabled these to be disguised as profits, a deception that continued until early 1995 when a spot check on the trader – clearly long overdue – revealed the true extent of the damage. While no one was watching, the bank had lost a sum more or less equal to its total assets.

The trader went on the run and then to jail. Dozens of senior executives resigned or were sacked and Barings itself was sold for a nominal £1 coin. Today all that remains is the Baring Archive, a fascinating trove of documents detailing more than two hundred years of international banking – or, if you prefer, a stark warning to all that in the City of London, not everyone's word is their bond.

The Battle of Assandun

Essex

A DECISIVE BATTLE BETWEEN ENGLAND AND Denmark on 18 October 1016, Cnut's crushing victory over Edmund II and his army marked the final chapter of the Vikings' reconquest of England.

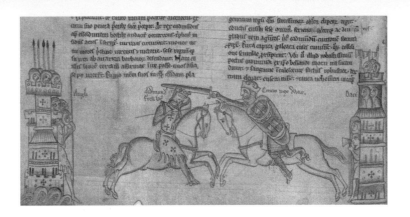

At least this much is fact, meaning that the date should surely be one of the most significant in English medieval history. That the battle also paved the way for the unification of England under a single king makes it even more extraordinary that most people don't know the date and no one is quite sure even where the fighting actually took place.

According to the twelfth-century historian John of Worcester: 'The armies fought obstinately, and many fell on both sides', until a traitor switched allegiance, thereby 'throwing victory to the Danes'. We know the defector was Eadric Streona, Ealdorman of Mercia and the son-in-law of the recently deceased Aethelred the Unready, yet the actual site of this treachery has been lost.

In Suffolk, a connection has been drawn between the battle and Assington, a quiet village near Sudbury; however, there is scant evidence for this theory and, as such, few subscribe to it. Instead, the manuscripts that make up the *Anglo-Saxon Chronicle* place Assandun further south, referring to the way Edmund gathered 'for the fifth time all the English nation, and went behind [the Danes] and overtook them in Essex'. The most favoured locations are Ashdon near Saffron Walden (in the north of the county) and Ashingdon, which is south-east towards the Thames.

Standing on the gentle slope of Ashingdon Hill today, it is certainly easy to imagine the troops assembling on either side. Indeed, the nearby village of Canewdon is often said to take its name from Cnut's camp.

Alas, this last point turns out not to be the case – the name 'Cana' probably refers to a local chieftain – so once again we have to be content with a few tantalizing details about the Vikings' triumph, and no real idea of where it was that Anglo-Saxon England died.

Blue Streak Silo

Cumberland

IN A LOST BID TO RETAIN A CREDIBLE INDEPENDENT nuclear deterrent, the country's first and last medium-range ballistic missile, Blue Streak, promised a bright future for British rocketry, but ultimately crashed and burned.

America's 1946 Atomic Energy Act placed restrictions on nuclear weapons sales to foreign governments; at the same time, Britain was keen to bolster its status as a major world power by developing its own. By 1955, however, it was apparent that the RAF's expensive V-Bomber fleet of Victors, Valiants and Vulcans would be obsolete within a decade, so a decision was taken to replace free-fall atomic weapons with missiles able to deliver destruction to an enemy under their own power.

With a target range of 1,500 nautical miles, or nearly

2,800 kilometres, the project brought together many of the biggest names in British armaments manufacturing, including de Havilland, Rolls Royce and the Atomic Weapons Research Establishment at Aldermaston. Ambitious consideration was also given to producing a three-stage version suitable for launching satellites into orbit.

Naturally, the scheme was not without its critics. These included anti-nuclear campaigners as well as Earl Mountbatten of Burma, who as Admiral of the Fleet unsurprisingly may have wished to see the Royal Navy supplant the RAF's greater popular appeal. There were also technical complications, such as the time taken to fuel each rocket immediately before its launch – loading more than eighty tonnes of kerosene and liquid oxygen took five minutes, leaving the Blue Streak potentially fatally exposed to a pre-emptive strike.

One answer was to site the rockets underground in hardened silos able to withstand a one-megaton explosion at a distance of half a mile. This exceptionally neat concept is one most closely associated with the Americans, although it was devised by the British, yet nothing seemed to have been done in terms of putting the idea into action.

For years there wasn't any evidence to suggest work on excavating silos had ever begun but, in 2004, tree-felling at RAF Spadeadam revealed traces of an abandoned prototype known as U1. It was a long way short of readiness, and no documentation about it has survived, but it is now believed to have been one of sixty launch sites planned for secret, isolated locations around the country.

Unfortunately, the silo plan was abandoned because, as the cost of Blue Streak rose from £50 million to £300 million to a projected £1.3 billion, it became apparent just how far Britain had slipped behind America and the USSR.

In 1960, the project was cancelled for good and, to the delight of Lord Mountbatten, Britain's modest submarine fleet was told to expect the first consignment of US-built Polaris missiles.

One surviving Blue Streak rocket is on display at the National Space Centre in Leicester, with another at Scotland's National Museum of Flight.

Borley Rectory

Suffolk

Famously 'the most haunted house in England', this otherwise unremarkable Gothic Revival vicarage was demolished in 1944, yet the legend has continued to grow.

The first reported manifestation at Borley was no more than a sound of footsteps, but in 1900 four of the Reverend Bull's fourteen children sighted a strange figure at twilight. Speculation as to the figure's identity landed on a medieval nun who was bricked up after being found *in flagrante* with a monk from a nearby Benedictine monastery.

That the story had no basis in fact seemed to bother no one, nor did the similarities the children's version bore to a couple of Victorian bestsellers by Henry Rider Haggard and Sir Walter Scott. Before long there were reports of headless horsemen and phantom coaches in the surrounding lanes, as well as the usual unexplained lights and servants' bells ringing after they had been disconnected.

In 1929, a reporter from the *Daily Mirror* arrived on the scene, and it was at this point that the Borley legend really took off. The paper also engaged Harry Price, a conjuror and self-styled psychical researcher, to investigate. He was soon describing textbook poltergeist activity – stones and bottles being thrown around and messages being tapped out on a mirror frame.

His report and the subsequent book made him famous, but they also attracted accusations of fraud and suggestions that he had been hoodwinked by rivals from the Society for Psychical Research. The Society certainly made every effort to have him taken off the case, and the vicar's wife later said the phenomena Price had recorded had ceased when he left, leading her to suppose he had faked them.

Claims of strange goings-on nevertheless continued – more than 2,000 of them by 1937, according to the BBC. As newspaper articles and books about the house piled up, nothing seemed to quell the level of interest in the place, not even the publication in 2000 of *We Faked the Ghosts of Borley Rectory* by Louis Mayerling. A frequent visitor to the house between the First and Second World Wars, the author described his involvement in various pranks and put-up jobs and a family who took an active delight in perpetuating local rumours about the house and its history.

The reality of Borley is perhaps simply that it has never been in anyone's interest to debunk the stories. Mayerling's book describes busloads of tourists, many from overseas with money to spend, and the demolition of the house after a fire in 1939, which ensured the story would run and run. With nowhere left to investigate, people could believe what they liked.

Borstals

Kent

SEPARATING YOUNG OFFENDERS FROM RECIDIVIST CAREER **criminals, borstals were meant to educate rather than punish, but rapidly became a byword for brutality among inmates and supervising staff.**

The brainchild of the chairman of the Prison Commission, Sir Evelyn Ruggles-Brise, the borstal was an attempt to implement the recommendations of the 1895 Gladstone Commission. This highlighted the need to reform young delinquents as well as deter them from committing future crimes, and Sir Evelyn proposed a new focus on routine, discipline and authority, with lessons and work placed at the heart of the inmates' time inside.

The scope for corporal punishment was also severely curtailed. From now on, the treadmill and crank were banned and birching of inmates would be permitted solely on the orders of a visiting magistrate, and even then only in cases of assaults on staff or mutiny. As a result, incidents of birching became extremely rare – far rarer than in the leading public schools of the time – although people now tend to assume the reverse.

The name of the new institutions came from a village near Rochester in Kent, because in October 1902 the first of them opened at Borstal Prison (now HM Prison Rochester). The inmates were aged sixteen to twenty-one and each day followed an unvarying timetable: a 6 a.m. start followed by a two-mile run with no breakfast for those who lagged behind. Food was basic, and tasks such as cleaning and cooking were carried out by inmates, who were also taught skills such as reading, writing, bricklaying and sewing.

Visitors were discouraged and privileges were only slowly introduced. These included ping pong, darts and cards in the evenings and, like breakfast, any entitlement was dependent on good behaviour.

It seems incredible now that the sentences were indeterminate, meaning an inmate was freed not after some specified time but only when it appeared that he or she had improved. Nor was everyone rehabilitated, as some inmates escaped and many went on to prison. However, a majority emerged better equipped for life and physically much fitter than before, which may well be more than can be said for the relatively relaxed regimes of the Young Offender Institutions that replaced borstals in 1983.

Braunstone Park Tunnels

Leicester

WHEN A GANG OF HOOLIGANS ARMED WITH A PNEUMATIC drill broke into the grounds of a handsome but neglected Georgian gem, they stumbled upon a lost network of mysterious underground tunnels.

Among the worst fates to befall an historical building is to be encircled by a housing estate and taken over by the local authority. Very few councils have the financial resources needed to maintain such places, and fewer still any clue as to what to do with them. One such site was once pleasantly located in the ancient hunting grounds of Leicester Forest.

In 1776, the Winstanley family built Braunstone Park and continued to live there until its compulsory purchase in 1926. Most of the grounds were then built over, with a portion set aside as a public park, and except for a short period when it was requisitioned by Allied forces stationed in the area, the red-brick hall spent much of the next seventy years as a school.

The pupils moved out in 1996, and ever since the Grade II-listed mansion has struggled to find a purpose. Boarded up and much dilapidated, at the time of writing it was being offered for sale on a long lease in the council's hope that it could be restored for use as a hotel and conference venue.

In their relatively isolated surroundings, buildings like this frequently prove irresistible to the bad and bored and, as such, Braunstone is not the first to attract the attention of vandals and arsonists. For once, however, the miscreants appear to have found something fascinating; something that had escaped the notice of its custodians for more than seventy years.

In 2011, local paper *Leicester Mercury* noted that a series of tunnels had been discovered running beneath the park. Reportedly steel-lined, suggesting they had nothing to do with the Winstanleys, they are now believed to have been constructed by US Air Force 86 Airborne Division personnel during the Second World War.

Described as bomb-proof corridors, rather than bunkers or air-raid shelters, the network must have allowed troops to move around safely during raids, but for security reasons it has since been sealed off again. As an interesting chapter in the history of this old house – and one shared by many others around the country – the hope must be that the tunnels will one day be restored along with poor, sad Braunstone Hall.

The Bristol Brabazon

East Lothian

CONCEIVED DURING THE SECOND WORLD WAR
but rapidly overtaken by the march of time,
exciting plans for a futuristic intercontinental
airliner used the blueprints of a stillborn
superbomber, yet suffered a similar fate.

When the Bristol Aeroplane Company was asked by a government committee to produce a luxurious new airliner, they sought out the 1943 designs for a strategic bomber with a range of more than 5,000 miles and a wingspan of 68.5 metres.

The bomber never took off but it would have been a true behemoth, with twice the range of the now legendary Avro Lancaster and longer wings than a Boeing 747. The development team at Bristol had immense faith in the idea and began working on an even larger machine for civilian use.

With a 54-metre-long fuselage and 70-metre wingspan, it was to be powered by eight gigantic 18-cylinder radial engines driving more than 21,000 horsepower through four pairs of counter-rotating propellers. Pressurized and air-conditioned, it was designed to be the first aircraft in the world to have a fully powered flight deck, electric engine controls and high-pressure hydraulics.

Its size and complexity called for a new factory to be built and a new, strengthened 2,400-metre runway, requiring the village of Chilton to be swept away and the residents removed to a nearby council estate.

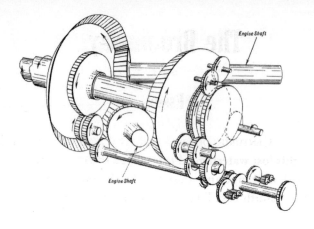

On 4 September 1949, the prototype lifted off for the first time. To the sound of cheering from thousands lining the runway, G-APGW made a few short circuits before landing. In the coming months she made appearances at Heathrow and the Paris Air Show but, despite the excitement, it was soon clear that the project was doomed.

Though huge and heavy, the swan-like Brabazon could seat only a few dozen people. Admittedly it did so in great comfort, but demand was already moving towards mass transport, not luxury for the few. Its immense radial engines were likewise outclassed by new turboprop and then jet airliners, rival designs that cut flight times dramatically and could carry far greater numbers.

With £6 million spent and not a single airline interested, in 1953 the project was terminated and the prototype sold as scrap. Barely anything has survived besides a couple of wheels and the front undercarriage leg. Displayed, Dodo-like, at the National Museum of Flight near East Fortune, the latter is a curiously poignant reminder of just how big this thing must have been.

The Broomway

Essex

CENTURIES OLD BUT LARGELY UNKNOWN,
**this lost waterlogged track links the mainland
with a strange and unearthly landscape in one of
south-east England's loneliest corners.**

For well over a thousand years, a six-mile walk across treacherous tidal sands was the only way to reach Foulness without a boat. It took until 1922 for marshy Havengore Creek[2] to be bridged, but members of the public still need permission to visit the island, which has been in military occupation since the Great War.

The local George and Dragon was probably the only pub in England where customers had to telephone ahead. No call meant no drink, and in 2007 it closed for the last time. The church went the same way three years later, but a village shop and post office still serve a small civilian population and any military personnel employed on the firing range.

The bridge means no one now uses the Broomway, although locally it is assumed to be so ancient that it predates an even earlier occupation, that of Roman legionaries. Its name is certainly old and refers to bundles of sticks tied to the poles, which used to mark the path's route at low tide.

Crossing to Foulness this way was legal but dangerous, and still is today. With the poles long gone, there is absolutely

2. The name comes from the Old English *haefen gor* ('muddy anchorage') and gave its name to the vessel that carried the body of Sir Winston Churchill along the Thames on 30 January 1965.

nothing marking the right of way and, leaving the mainland at Wakering Stairs, it is far easier to lose one's bearings than to stay on the path. The tide is the biggest danger (it comes in at a terrifying rate and seemingly from every direction), while signs warn visitors against touching or even approaching objects that 'MAY EXPLODE AND KILL YOU'.

A large-scale map is therefore essential, together with a compass and a tide timetable. But even if well equipped, and allowing three hours to walk out and back, the adventure should really only be undertaken by those experienced in navigation, or in the company of someone who has walked this way before.

Cable Railway

Derbyshire

Evolution rarely proceeds in a straight line, meaning some of Britain's earliest railways ran for years without seeing a single, conventional steam locomotive.

With the internal combustion engine taken for granted, it seems astonishing now that the first car to beat 100 mph was powered by steam or that London had a fleet of seventy electric taxicabs as long ago as 1897.

Both soon turned out to be no more than a technological dead end and similarly novel ideas were frequently tried on the railways, too, before being found wanting. Areas such as the Derbyshire Peak District were especially challenging to the pioneers; somewhere a new railway might promise a faster way to transport goods than by road or canal, but only if the terrain could be conquered.

One of the first ever long-distance lines, the Cromford and High Peak Railway was constructed in 1831 to haul minerals rather than passengers the more than thirty miles between the Cromford and Peak Forest canals. Climbing above 380 metres – higher than any English mainline today – the route took in several steep inclines, the worst of which was a 1-in-7 slope (14.3 per cent).

No conventional locomotive could cope with such a gradient, so the operators decided to use stationary winding engines: huge steam-powered monsters built by the Butterley Company of Ripley.[3] These cable-hauled the wagons along each incline while teams of horses were roped in for the flatter sections. Progress along the primitive fishbelly rails was slow, and completing the journey typically took two whole days.

Fixed engines had other drawbacks, too. Their best hemp rope frayed with alarming rapidity; chains were too heavy and even the best steel cables had a tendency to kink. Runaway wagons weighed down with stone were also a clear danger, hence the rather alarming emergency 'catch pit' that can still be seen beneath the A6 trunk road.

Failing ever to turn a profit, the line closed eventually and after the rails were torn up in the 1970s much of it was incorporated into the National Cycle Network. However, near Middleton-by-Wirksworth, enthusiasts have rescued the last surviving pair of beam engines, which are occasionally fired up for demonstrations.

---

3. See Fritchley Tunnel (page 55) for more on this company, which survived until 2009 and supplied the metal for Vauxhall Bridge in London, the Falkirk Wheel and Portsmouth's Spinnaker Tower.

Chariot Racing

Essex

AS SPORTS GO, CHARIOT RACING SEEMS AS
traditionally Roman as throwing Christians to
lions, yet there was once a racetrack dedicated to
this classical activity in Essex – the only one of its
kind in the British Isles.

The Romans made their capital at Camulodunum, meaning
the place we call Colchester has been a garrison town for longer
than anywhere in Europe. With the army reducing in size in
recent years, however, the Ministry of Defence has sold much
of its land for development and the track came to light as part
of this process, during excavations on a site that (appropriately)
had hitherto been occupied by cavalry barracks.

Archaeologists initially thought they had found temple
remains and began to suspect it was a racetrack only after
a visitor joked about finding a chariot. The suspicion was
confirmed when Colchester's measurements were compared

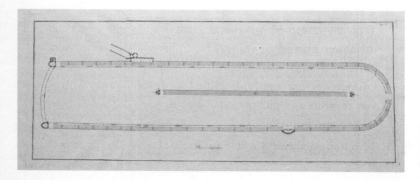

to drawings of a similar site in Spain and found to be almost identical.

Lost beneath roads, gardens and military buildings, the second-century structure is thought to have been large enough to accommodate as many as 15,000 spectators. At five metres tall, 400 long and 69 wide, it may well have been the largest Roman building in the country after Hadrian's Wall.

Unfortunately, nothing has survived above ground, and not that much below. But following a successful campaign locally, part of the site is to be preserved and, once funds allow, it should form the centrepiece of a unique archaeological park in Britain's oldest recorded town.

Cockfighting

Glamorgan

UNTIL IT WAS OUTLAWED IN ENGLAND AND WALES in 1835,[4] cockfighting had enjoyed a long run as the world's oldest spectator sport with a history dating back as far as 6,000 years.

Typically assumed to characterize the brutal tastes of the lower classes, in reality the fights and the gambling associated with them appealed to all. One visitor to a London cockpit neatly described the attendant crowd he saw as 'peers and pickpockets, grooms and gentlemen, *bon vivants* and bullies'.

---

4. Scottish enthusiasts were able to avoid the ban for another sixty years.

Male birds are naturally aggressive to other males and with vulnerabilities such as wattles and combs removed, their wings clipped and vicious spurs fitted, a pair of gamecocks will instinctively fight each other until one or both is mortally wounded. The result is as bloody and awful as it sounds, but with high entry fees, huge wagers and prized birds raised on bizarre diets of raw meat, maggots and even urine, so many different vested interests ensured the cruel sport had a long and lucrative history.

By the eighteenth century, most towns and villages in Britain had at least one cockpit and big cities boasted many, but today they have nearly all gone. Of a handful of survivors, the best is at St Fagans National History Museum at Cardiff: a carefully restored small stone building, circular with a conical thatched roof.

Without knowing anything of its horrible history, it could readily be mistaken for a charming tollhouse or a picturesque dovecote. Known to date from the seventeeth century, and now Grade II-listed, it was taken there in 1965 after being rescued from the yard of the Hawk and Buckle Inn at Denbigh. Having spent many years as a car workshop, and a few as a pig weighstation, it is now almost impossible to imagine its original purpose.

Condemned Cell

London

THE MURDER (ABOLITION OF DEATH Penalty) Act passed into UK law in 1965, but it's a matter of record that nearly thirty years later at least one set of gallows was still in situ. More incredibly, it was still being checked by Wandsworth prison staff every six months to ensure the moving parts were in working order.

The scaffold at the grim south-London prison was only finally dismantled in 1994, and today all that is left of it are a few ghoulish items such as ankle-straps, the trapdoor and a hangman's lever. These are on display alongside Oscar Wilde's cell door at the Galleries of Justice Museum in Nottingham.

The condemned cell itself is still intact, however, although it has been converted into a television lounge for the prison guards. It is slightly larger than a conventional cell, and has two doors rather than one. The second opened directly onto the execution chamber, although there is nothing to suggest this today and even when it was used for its original purpose it is likely that none of the 135 individuals who spent their final few

hours locked up here had any idea how close he or she was sitting to their eventual nemesis.

The 135 were not the last to be hanged in England: Gwynne Evans and Peter Allen achieved that distinction on 13 August 1964 when they were hanged simultaneously at Manchester and Liverpool for battering a van driver to death. But the Wandsworth cell saw many far more notorious prisoners, not a few of whose executions continue to arouse controversy even among those who think the death penalty is a good thing.

They include William Joyce, for example, the Nazi radio propagandist known as 'Lord Haw-Haw', who carved a swastika into his cell wall in 1946. An awful piece of work, he was nevertheless an American citizen, not a British one, and assumed German nationality in 1940, thereby making the charge against him of treason something of a nonsense in a British court.

Another was Derek Bentley, who was executed in 1953 after the murder of a policeman in Croydon. PC Sidney Miles had been shot dead by Bentley's accomplice, yet Christopher Craig escaped execution because he was only sixteen at the time. Instead, Lord Chief Justice Goddard arranged for Bentley to pay the price in what now looks like a chillingly expedient response to public demands for revenge.

The same could be said of the Joyce hanging as well, of

course, but perhaps the most disgraceful thing about Britain's judiciary is the contrast between the speed with which it moved when hanging the accused and the quite incredible sloth evident when it comes to overturning even the grossest miscarriages. Despite being assessed by the very court that hanged him as 'feeble-minded', Bentley was executed just a fortnight after his first appeal. Securing a full pardon for their dead son was to take his family more than forty-five years.

Coquet Stop Line

Northumberland

As many as 28,000 pillboxes were hastily thrown up in the weeks following the Dunkirk debacle. Often appearing to have been plonked down at random, the truth is that there was a plan, although it can be hard to discern now that so many have disappeared.

Pillbox was the word the public used to describe the most visible components of what the armed forces preferred to call hardened field defences. These formed a key part of anti-invasion preparations intended to halt or at least delay the progress of invading Germans.

Besides pillboxes and trenches, a variety of concrete pimples, cones, cubes and cylinders were employed to impede the advance of tracked and wheeled vehicles. Much of the effort was concentrated in the south-east and around London (see GHQ Line, page 62), but so-called stop lines were also created further north, including Northumberland.

Taking its title from the river of the same name, the Coquet Stop Line ran inland from Amble, Northumberland. Following the valley of the river, it was constructed to give defenders time to assemble and prepare their defences on another stop line thirty miles further south on the Tyne.

The urgent need to build so many pillboxes in such a short time meant the job was largely contracted out, often using relatively unskilled labour. Considerable variation in pillbox design and quality resulted: the lozenge shape found on the Coquet being unique to this part of the country.[5] Essentially a stretched hexagon, they have four gun embrasures on the long front face and one in each of the four short end walls. The entrance is at the rear, concealed behind a blast wall or low porch.

Despite the robustness of their construction, several have been lost or destroyed and one at least is subsiding badly due to the action of the river. However, most survive. Originally they were placed at approximately two-mile intervals and today, with around twenty of the miniature fortresses still standing, it is possible to plot the line's course from Rothbury to West Thirston.

Together they make a melancholy reminder of very dark days, a strange legacy from a time when Britain really did stand alone. With no regard to anything but function, they are ugly but important nevertheless, and surely deserve a better fate than being allowed just to crumble back into the landscape.

---

5. Lozenge-shaped boxes are also found in Essex, but while at first glance these appear similar, they are octagonal.

Croydon Canal

Surrey

**IF OLD PILLBOXES SPEAK OF A CERTAIN DOGGED
defiance, the short-lived Croydon Canal tells a
story of an entirely different sort of hope.**

By providing carriers with a new waterway from West Epsom
in Surrey to the Thames at Rotherhithe, the Croydon Canal
Company expected to grow fat on the profits of transporting
vast quantities of building stone, lime and timber at a time
when the capital was expanding faster than ever.

A fleet of twenty-two huge eighteen-metre barges was
commissioned to carry up to thirty tonnes apiece, and
plans drawn up for two inclined planes. As a means of
raising the boats from one water level to another, these were
sophisticated but expensive and eventually the company
was forced to settle instead for a more conventional series
of locks.

These were cheaper to build, but much slower to
navigate as twenty-eight sets were needed. Keeping the locks
full required huge quantities of water, meaning the company
also had to excavate two new reservoirs at Sydenham and
South Norwood. (The latter, covering nearly a dozen
hectares, is now home to numerous monster carp.)

Despite this impressive investment in infrastructure,
the canal progressed barely half the planned distance before
work stopped. In this truncated form it struggled on for only
twenty-seven years following its 1809 inauguration. When
£100 shares in the company slumped to just 2/- (or 10p), it

became the only canal in the country ever to be closed by a special Act of Parliament.

At Anerley, an attempt was made to turn a short stretch of it into an attractive boating lake with tea rooms and pleasant walks. But this too proved insufficiently popular and, with shareholders desperate to recoup some of their losses, the land was sold off. Most of it went to the London & Croydon Railway Company, a bitter pill for the project's promoters to swallow as it was the coming of the railways that had killed their canal and later so many others.

Today, visitors to Anerley can still walk around a slightly melancholy rectangular pond in Betts Park, and a piece of towpath has survived as a curious raised stretch of pavement in David's Road, Forest Hill. Otherwise, the best way to follow the route of the old canal is to catch the London Bridge commuter service from West Croydon and use your imagination.

Dirigibles

Bedfordshire

**AMONG THE LARGEST BUILDINGS ANYWHERE IN
Europe, two vast sheds on the outskirts of
Bedford are a slightly mournful memorial to a
lost dream of elegant, transcontinental travel.**

Together with the model village of Shortstown for company
workers, the first 210-metre-long hangar was built in 1915
as a private venture by the aircraft pioneers, Short Brothers.
Called No.1 Shed, it housed two early vessels, HMA *R31* and
R32, which were designed by the Admiralty with help from a
German defector named Herr Müller.

Equipped with defensive machine guns and an underslung
12-pounder gun for use on submarines, these 187-metre
dirigibles were expected to join airborne fleet protection
patrols. However, they entered service too late to be of use and
the operation was nationalized soon after the Armistice.

The newly named Royal Airship Works then expanded
rapidly. No.1 Shed was extended to almost 250 metres and a
second hangar acquired from the Royal Navy Air Station at
Pullham in Norfolk was re-erected next to it. Work then turned
to the construction of a new, much larger vessel, the *R101*,
designed for long-distance passenger transport to the furthest
corners of the British Empire.

At just over 236 metres, this was the largest aircraft the
world had ever seen and was produced in tandem with a rival
design, *R100*, from a team of privateers including Barnes Wallis
(of 'Dambuster' fame) and the novelist Nevil Shute. The hope

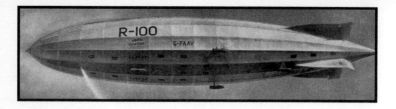

was to combine the lessons from both and to create an elite squadron of Imperial airships able to fly to Canada in three days, India in six and Australia in no more than ten.

It was not to be. Cosseting passengers in luxury, described as midway between a Pullman car and an ocean liner,[6] the *R100* successfully crossed to North America, but in October 1930, en route to India, its sister ship crashed on the edge of a wood in Picardy, northern France. Forty-eight passengers and crew died and although airship enthusiasts continue to debate the causes of the tragedy, it spelled the death of official attempts in this country to design and build lighter-than-air machines.

A few scraps of metal were salvaged from the wreckage and fashioned into ashtrays. The rest was sold to a company founded by the German Count Ferdinand von Zeppelin, which went on to build the even larger LZ 129 *Hindenburg*. The *R100* had

6. First-class facilities included a smoking room, despite the millions of litres of hydrogen sitting just above the smokers' heads.

been confined to her hangar immediately following the tragedy and now she too was broken up. It took a while: eleven miles of metal tubing, several acres of fabric and animal intestines for the gas bags, and more than five million rivets.

The hangars happily survived and, under the auspices of RAF Cardington, both found new uses when another war with Germany called for the construction of thousands of tethered barrage balloons, or blimps, to guard against aerial attack. Later still, another form of balloon took flight from here, when the Royal Aircraft Establishment used No.1 Shed as a base from which to launch weather balloons carrying instruments to measure atmospheric conditions on behalf of the Met Office.

Twice since, attempts have been made to rekindle interest in airships, most recently with something called the HAV Airlander. Described as the world's longest aircraft (although it is less than half the length of the *R101*), it has aroused nothing like the same sense of public excitement, and at the time of writing its success or lack thereof has still to be determined.

Doggerland

Norfolk

One could walk from England to Germany until approximately 8,000 years ago, when rising sea levels led to the loss of the landmass that made it possible.

It seems extraordinary now, but far from being just a simple land bridge, the area known as Doggerland was settled by

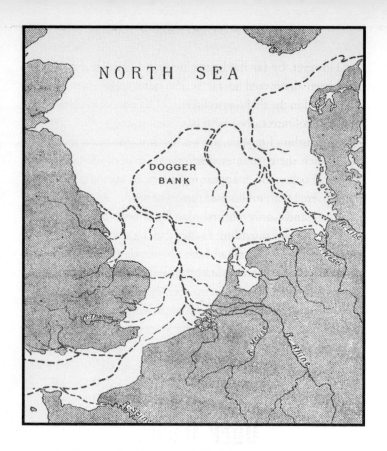

mankind as well as animals before being swamped by the North Sea. Trawlers occasionally dredge up evidence for this, including the remains of mammoths and primeval big cats and – if only very rarely – primitive tools made by early man.

The precise timing and cause of Doggerland's disappearance is still to be determined, but it will have been some time after the last Ice Age, probably as a result of climate change or even a mega-tsunami. Finds hauled from the depths have included flint tools and a barbed antler, which was most likely used as a sort of harpoon. A single piece of Neanderthal skull has also been brought up, although this was found close to the Dutch coast.

However, by far the largest remnant of the lost land to have been discovered so far is an entire prehistoric forest, submerged in the shallows as little as 200 metres off a Norfolk beach. A volunteer diver who has been exploring this stretch of the coastline for years, Dawn Watson, made the find in 2014 when she encountered several giant trees – probably a species of oak – which appear to have been knocked flat and then covered with millions of tonnes of sand.

The sands only shifted during recent severe storm activity, thereby providing modern man's first glimpse of a region of Europe that had been colonized by our hunter-gatherer forebears. Dendrochronologists (scientists who use the technique of dating events, environmental change and archaeological artefacts by using growth rings in timber and tree trunks) have since dated the wood to around 10,000 years old, although no more evidence of human habitation has come to light.

Duck Decoy

Buckinghamshire

IN LONDON AT LOW TIDE IT IS STILL POSSIBLE TO find traces of Saxon fish and eel traps in the Thames, and near Brill in Buckinghamshire the National Trust has preserved what might be described as their avian equivalent.

Today the word decoy has a wider meaning, but its origins are Dutch and originally described a type of wicker

enclosure introduced to Britain from the Netherlands in the seventeenth century.[7] After landing on a lake or pond, waterfowl were encouraged into these enclosures by dogs specially trained for the purpose.

The ruse works because ducks can become victims of their own curiosity. Faced with a likely predator, a duck will often keep it under observation rather than fly away. Mistaking a hunter's dog for a fox, birds could thus be tricked into remaining on the water and gently led along the course of the decoy. Thereafter, the chances of escape would be reduced by narrowing the width of the enclosure as the birds paddled farther into it, and by giving it a curved shape that cut off the view of the pond.

Once trapped in this way, the birds could be easily caught and killed; the meat all the better for being free of lead shot.

As a source of nutrition, the decoys proved relatively

7. Another type of decoy, a floating model duck, is nowadays used by hunters to lure real birds onto the water.

cheap and efficient and soon hundreds were being constructed around the country. By the late nineteenth century, however, the number had slumped to a few dozen and today there are just four which, if they are used at all, play a role in trapping animals for ringing rather than for the pot.

Hidden away in woodland, the Boarstall duck decoy is beautifully preserved and fairly typical of the late seventeenth century, although iron hoops suggest it might have been of above-average quality. With three separate enclosures or 'pipes', it includes hurdles behind which the decoyman could hide, perhaps throwing grain onto the surface of the water to further tempt the birds to their doom.

Originally serving the kitchens of a now-vanished medieval manor house – to which the National Trust's Boarstall Tower is the old gatehouse – this simple but ingenious device remained in use until the 1940s.

Duns

Berwickshire

DUNS STILL EXISTS, BUT BENEATH AN AREA OF THE town known as the Bruntons or 'burned towns' lies the original medieval settlement.

It is impossible to pinpoint the first ever cross-border battle, but the history of Anglo–Scottish skirmishes is a long one, and the boundary between the two countries is conceivably the world's oldest.

Its course was established in law by the Treaty of York in 1327, but territorial disputes continued for another 250 years, just as they had for at least the previous 650. Towns closest to the line naturally suffered the most – Berwick-on-Tweed famously changing hands many times over several centuries.[8] Duns, Berwickshire's historic county town, was ransacked no fewer than three times in succession. Levelled in 1544, 1545 and then again in 1588, the decision was finally taken to rebuild from scratch on a completely new site.

Originally an Iron Age fort on the slopes of a hill called Duns Law, Duns was already a thriving place in the early twelfth century, and the Franciscan philosopher Scotus was later born here in 1265–6. Unfortunately, its strategically important hilltop position overlooking the Cheviots meant it was frequently attacked or garrisoned by English troops marching north – in 1372, the population successfully routed a force of 7,000, achieved by frightening their horses using an array of bird-scarers and homemade rattles.

This home win was a rare one, however. When Duns was made a burgh of barony by James IV in 1490 – conferring on the local landowner the rights to hold a weekly market and an annual fair – it served only to make the town a more obvious target to raiders.

In particular, Duns fell victim to the Rough Wooing, that period from late 1543 that saw Henry VIII attempt to bully the Scots into accepting a marriage between his son Edward and the one-year-old Mary Stuart, their future queen. With French support courtesy of the Auld Alliance, Scotland successfully resisted, but as King Edward VI, the son continued the fight after his father's death.

8. English from 1482, it was only fully incorporated into Northumberland in 1885.

Today the earthworks of the aforementioned Iron Age fort are a popular destination for walkers on Duns Law, and in 1966 Franciscan monks erected a small cairn on the site of the house where Scotus was born. It is therefore possible to establish where Duns once stood, but it is remarkable how completely the traces of an entire town have disappeared.

Eaton Hall

Cheshire

THE TWENTIETH CENTURY WITNESSED THE DELIBERATE destruction of more than 1,500 large country houses, many hundreds of which are now recognized to have been of considerable architectural significance.

Among the most grievous of the losses was the seat of the dukes of Westminster, although the reasons for its demolition in the 1960s are not hard to grasp.

The third and by far the largest of five houses – which had until then provided a central focus for this large and conspicuously well-run rural estate – was built for the first duke, Hugh Grosvenor, by Alfred Waterhouse. Beginning in 1870, it took the architect of the Natural History Museum and Manchester Town Hall twelve years to complete, costing his client around £800,000, or more than twice as much as London's much-loved St Pancras Station, its near contemporary.

Enclosing the core of an earlier Georgian house, which a young Queen Victoria found magnificent on her first visit,

His Grace opted for Gothic Revival, the highly fashionable style of which Waterhouse was a master. In Eaton Hall he created something huge and strikingly original, a building the architectural historian Nikolas Pevsner described as the most ambitious of its kind anywhere in the country. More recently it has been characterized as *Gormenghastly*, but typically by those who know it only from postcards.

Old black and white photographs at least give a good impression of its size. Besides 150 bedrooms and a fifty-five-metre clock tower with a twenty-eight-bell carillon, the library was nearly thirty metres long and the dining room larger still. Viewed from the far side of the park's spectacular Golden Gates, the hall may have looked more like a Victorian public school than a family home (it was larger than many of the more famous stately homes), but the interior provided a magnificent, gilded backdrop to what is still one of Europe's greatest private art collections.

Following the hall's requisition as a hospital in both world wars, the second, third and fourth dukes seemed content for it to remain in government hands. For three years Eaton was home to Britannia Royal Naval College, which had been bombed out of Dartmouth in 1942, and the training of officer cadets continued here until National Service came to an end in 1958, when it finally returned to the Grosvenor fold.

Badly knocked about, full of dry rot, horribly expensive to maintain and needing armies of indoor and outdoor servants to function, it was emphatically not what the childless fourth duke needed in the 1960s. A more impecunious family might have tried to give it away, but it is by no means certain that the National Trust could have afforded the upkeep. In any case, as the owner of hundreds of acres of central London, the Grosvenors were not poor, and after five centuries at Eaton they could be forgiven for not wishing to see day-trippers wandering around their more than seventeen-square-mile demesne.

Accordingly, in 1963, work began to dismantle what the *Daily Telegraph* called 'one of the most princely and beautiful mansions that these islands contain'. Soon only the immense stable block, chapel and clock tower were left standing, together with the lodges and the aforementioned Grade I-listed gates. Behind these a new Eaton Hall was soon under construction – one which continues to be lived in and loved by the family.

Elizabethan Horology

City of London

IN 1912, WORKMEN DISCOVERED A **priceless collection of nearly 500 Elizabethan and Jacobean jewels. The haul included an astonishing timepiece that suggested a level of sophistication nearly four centuries ago that continues to baffle watchmakers even now.**

Known as the Cheapside Hoard, the gems and jewels were discovered during demolition work on an old cellar, perhaps after being buried under the floor by a goldsmith who was fearful of losing his stock during the Civil War. By far the most impressive find of its kind anywhere in Europe, the array of Roman gems, necklaces, rings, bodkins, beads and Byzantine cameos has since added immeasurably to our knowledge of life and trade in London prior to the Great Fire, when so much was lost.

The navvies sold the items to a shady pawnbroker

nicknamed Stony Jack, quite illegally, and for a fraction of their value. He in turn arranged for them to be displayed in the new London Museum, acting just as illegally and in exchange for official recognition and a new role as the City's Inspector of Excavations. Greasing the wheels was a Liberal MP who was later made a viscount, leaving everyone happy with the arrangement except the cellar owners – the Worshipful Company of Goldsmiths – and the British Museum, which had hoped to acquire the lot.

Ownership by a public body has at least meant that over the last hundred years every item has been subjected to the minutest scrutiny. Besides the self-evident quality of the collection, perhaps the most outstanding feature is how international it is. Underlining London's pre-eminence as a centre for global trade, expert study of the jewels has uncovered examples of stones, metalwork and craftsmanship from almost every corner of the world.

The aforementioned watch, for example, is set within a large Colombian emerald, brilliantly cut and hollowed out to accommodate movement, the workings of which are still not understood. Another is signed by a maker who was working in Geneva between 1610 and 1620.

As well as Burmese rubies and Persian turquoise, jewels from the hoard have been traced to India (diamonds), the Arabian Gulf (pearls), Ceylon (moonstones), Italy (lapis lazuli) and China (nephrite jade). Surprisingly, the collection includes just one fake, but even this has an international dimension and is thought to have been created using ingenious tricks devised by a Florentine glassworker based in Antwerp.

England's Atlantis

Suffolk

WITH MUCH OF IT ALL BUT INVISIBLE
beneath the murky waters of the North Sea,
Dunwich today has a population of around
800. This is well down from the 3,000 residents
estimated to have been living here at the time
of the Domesday survey, a size that would have
made it one of the dozen largest settlements
in England.

Popularly but erroneously said to have been engulfed overnight by a single biblical fourteenth-century storm, the decline of the once-thriving medieval port was a much slower and more gradual process. Indeed, many living close enough to the east coast can see for themselves its ongoing erosion and, in fact, the last of the town's eight churches survived until just after the Great War.

By then Dunwich had been under attack for at least 900 years, the damage caused almost entirely by storms and surges. The first reported loss of buildings came on New Year's Day, 1286, but land had been disappearing long before this. The following year saw two periods of extensive flooding: the first more or less wiped out Winchelsea in Sussex; both impacted heavily on Dunwich and neighbouring villages.

On both occasions, hundreds died on either side of the North Sea. However, the lasting effect was to redraw great stretches of the coastline. In the process, several navigable watercourses were permanently rerouted – in the case of the

Dunwich River so that its outlet to the sea shifted a couple of miles north to Walberswick.

Its sheltered harbour now useless, Dunwich quickly lost its economic impetus as a trading and fishing port. Revenues fell and people moved away: with no one to maintain its coastal defences, the town became more exposed than ever to the unceasing action of a cruel sea.

In 1347, as many as 400 houses fell victim to the waves – by this time many must have been uninhabited – and then in January 1362 came the *Grote Mandrenke*. Saxon for 'the Great Drowning', this cataclysmic event claimed as many as 25,000 English, Danish, Dutch and German lives[9] as seawater rushed miles inland. For Dunwich, its population already well down from its 5,000 peak, it was the last straw.

Further destruction occurred in 1560 and 1570; another storm in 1740 flattened almost all of what was left. Afterwards, just one church was left standing, although All Saints was a ruin years before its final disappearance in 1919.

Over a pint in The Ship they'll tell you that sometimes you can still hear the bells from those lost church towers, and it's true that, having mapped all of its underwater streets and lanes, Dunwich is only a very short distance offshore. But, unfortunately, surveys can be carried out only by using advanced sonar and other geophysical techniques. Swimming around a drowned city may sound wonderfully romantic, but England's Atlantis really is lost, and those who have dived down to take a look now know there is pitifully little left to see.

---

9. Many others too. (See Ravenser Odd, page 134)

The Flyers' Graveyard

Derbyshire

THERE ARE MANY HUNDREDS, EVEN thousands, of Second World War crash sites around Britain, ranging from a Hawker Hurricane lost for decades beneath a crossroads near Buckingham Palace, to the remains of an American military flying boat in a remote spot on Yell in Shetland.

The ruins of many aircraft were recovered and, wherever possible, pilots and aircrew were given a decent burial. But at the height of the war, manpower shortages made it impossible to retrieve what was often a mass of useless scrap, especially in cases where the wreckage was distributed over a large area or in an inaccessible location.

The latter was certainly true for much of the Peak District, a beautiful region but one that proved deadly for pilots in the 1940s. Young and inexperienced pilots frequently became disorientated above the cloud-covered peaks after long operations or in bad weather. Even the best found themselves struggling with aircraft fatally damaged by flak during missions to occupied Europe.

In all, the decade saw more than 120 aircraft plummet to the ground in this area, with the loss of 157 lives. Consequently, after seventy years, the hills are still strewn with often substantial pieces of metal, much of it melted by fire as the aircraft burned out of control or was twisted out of shape by the force of its impact with the ground.

Sometimes, horribly, trophy hunters steal and sell the items they find up there. At other sites walkers have piled them up into makeshift cairns, creating memorials to the dead that are untidy but in their own way honest and heartfelt. At still more, the remains have been left alone to corrode, slowly vanishing into rock crevices and peatbogs.

On its way back from bombing Liverpool in 1941, a Luftwaffe Junkers Ju88 came to grief on a ridge known as the Roaches (from the French for 'rocks') at the cost of four lives. The overwhelming majority of the Peak District dead were Allied airmen, however, including three Hurricane pilots at Tintwhistle Knarr, five members of the crew of a crippled Handley Page Halifax on Kinder Scout, and four from another Handley Page bomber lost over Cluther Rocks.

The most surprising loss is probably that of a USAF Boeing RB-29A Superfortress, similar to the ones that dropped the first atomic bombs on Hiroshima and Nagasaki. In theory, its advanced pressurized design meant it could fly far higher than most of its contemporaries, enabling it to steer clear of the hills. Alas, it came to grief in 1948, long after the war had ended, having got lost en route from Scampton in Lincolnshire to RAF Burtonwood.

Whatever the cause, thirteen crew were killed when the four-engined bomber ploughed into an area of Bleaklow's gritstone moor known as Higher Shelf Stones. Its engines, undercarriage and other large components can still be seen scattered widely across the haunting, windswept landscape, close to where a remembrance service is held each year.

Fritchley Tunnel

Derbyshire

LONDONERS LIKE TO BOAST ABOUT THE NORTHERN LINE being the longest railway tunnel in the world (which it was for a while), but the oldest was somehow lost until somebody found it hidden beneath a rockery.

The discovery was made in 2013, but the tunnel itself dates back more than 200 years to the late eighteenth century. Constructed in 1793, it formed part of a narrow-gauge railway running through the small hamlet of Fritchley near Crich. Used to haul newly quarried limestone down to barges on the Cromford Canal, it was known as the Butterley Gang Road and was horse-drawn until 1813, when steampower arrived in the county in the shape of the intriguing Brunton Mechanical Traveller.

The Traveller or 'Steam Horse' used a pair of rear-mounted legs to push itself along the rails, much like a skier with poles. It looks cumbersome and could move at no more than walking pace, but the technology proved reasonably successful until an improved version exploded two years later. Thirteen people were killed in the blast, making it the world's first recorded railway disaster.

The railway kept on working, however, and only closed in the mid-1930s when the eighteen-metre-long, stone-lined tunnel fell idle. For a few years during the war it was reopened and converted for use as an air-raid shelter, but again fell into disuse in 1945 when it was more or less forgotten about. It disappeared from view entirely when a Fritchley homeowner, wishing to build a rockery in his cottage garden, decided to seal up the entrance. This seems extraordinary now, but these were different times.

Locally, the Gang Road's history was well known and a couple of years ago a chance conversation with members of the county archaeological society resulted in a successful application for funds to begin digging. The entrance was found shortly afterwards, approximately three metres below the surface.

Damp but well preserved, the tunnel was expertly measured and mapped by laser, enabling a computer model to be made of it for future study. At that time, the oldest known railway tunnel was thought to be on the Peak Forest Railway (also in Derbyshire), but to the delight of the diggers, further research showed this one to date to a full two years earlier and, at the time of writing, it still holds the world record.

Intact but fragile and by no means easy to access, it has since been sealed again to protect it from damage or deterioration.

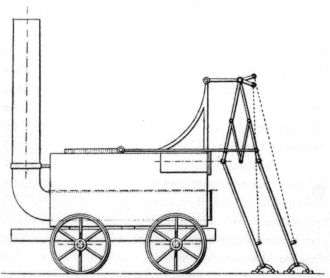

Gainsthorpe

Lincolnshire

**More than 3,000 deserted medieval villages
in Britain bear witness to the shifting patterns of
human habitation. Some were cleared to make way
for sheep, landscaped parks or monasteries; others
were depopulated by plague or war. But a few
cases are still shrouded in mystery, despite detailed
archaeology and years of study.**

Just two miles from Hibaldstow, the village of Gainsthorpe
falls into this category. Particularly from the air – it was first
identified by a former Royal Flying Corps observer – the layout
of the village is easy to discern by the humps and hollows of
the otherwise flat and low-lying Lincolnshire landscape.

Conveniently located for Ermine Street, the Roman
road running from London through Lincoln to York, its
three streets appear as sunken 'hollow ways'. These are edged
by an irregular pattern of small yards (or tofts) belonging to
individual stone-built properties, each one separated from
its neighbours by low banks with its narrow garden (or
croft) stretching out behind.

Not all of these smallholdings are readily distinguished,
but the village at its peak appears to have comprised around
thirty buildings, a mix of small two-room dwellings and larger
byres or barns. After so long, the walls are no more than low,
grass-covered foundations (once abandoned, much of the
stone would have been removed for building elsewhere), but
in many of them it is possible to see where the entrances would

have been. Some of the buildings also appear to have been knocked through – perhaps at a later date as the population thinned out and properties became vacant.

The number of dwellings mark Gainsthorpe out as quite a large village, and at various times a windmill and chapel were recorded, as well as a rectangular fishpond and two dovecotes. However, by 1616 it was noted that 'there is nowe neyther tofte, tenemente or cottage standinge [and that] it keepes neer 1,500 sheepe'.

One popular theory about the place is that it was intentionally cleared out after becoming a den of thieves. Almost certainly incorrect, this story is an old one: writing in 1697, a visiting curate called Abraham de la Pryme described being told how a 'pretty large town' had been demolished by long-suffering neighbours who had 'for a long while endur'd all their villanys'. Wisely he chose not to believe the tale, fancying instead that Gainsthorpe had 'been eaten up with time, poverty and pasturage'.

The likelihood is that de la Pryme was correct, at least in part. By the fourteenth century, feudalism was in retreat, giving many labourers the freedom to travel and seek work elsewhere. Wages also increased dramatically when the Black Death killed up to half the population, radically altering the accepted economic system. In particular, the sudden shortage of manpower from around 1350 forced rich landowners to hire and pay for labour rather than simply demanding it from an underclass that had no real negotiating power.

Tudor enclosures may also have played a role: this was the process by which landowners acquired great swathes of the countryside – often not doing so legally – and replaced arable farming with herds of sheep. One of the great economic drivers in medieval England, the large-scale production of woollen cloth, turned out to be far more profitable than raising crops – as well as requiring far fewer hands.

With little work and no land of their own, the villagers may have left to seek employment in the towns. Against this background, Gainsthorpe and many like it were clearly doomed, but with no records – and almost no archaeology on this particular site – questions about how, why and where they went are likely to remain unanswered.

Gasometers

THE VERY NAME IS A REMINDER OF JUST HOW OLD these not-so-shining examples of our industrial heritage are and, with hundreds having been dismantled, what were once ubiquitous will soon be a thing of the past.

The world's most-famous gas holder is the large, circular drum that peers over the stands at The Oval cricket ground in Kennington, south London, but it's doubtful many fans of the sport give a moment's thought to how it works, let alone whether or not it still does.

The first iron giant was built in 1824, bringing better lighting and heating to people. Coal or town gas was made on site by burning coal and then pumping it into these vast containers. Each one could be up to seventy metres in diameter and almost as tall, with another ten metres or more reaching down into the ground.

In busy areas the drums would rise and fall almost daily as the gas was pumped in and then used up, a feature that

has been likened to a heart beating on a city scale. This gave them their slightly enigmatic character, and children in particular would marvel at the mysterious way in which an apparently solid mass had disappeared the next day, becoming a slender lattice of struts and poles.

Pressurized North Sea gas changed all this and, along with a better understanding of fluctuating demand patterns, these gaunt giants gradually fell into disuse. A handful of the older, more decorative ones have been listed and will survive; more will become arts centres or even blocks of flats. But with more than 550, the National Grid has been struggling for years with the maintenance requirements of so much old metal, so a sell-off has always been a possibility.

These days, the inner-city sites that they occupy are dangerous places, but also hugely valuable. Although dismantling each gasometer takes months and costs around a million pounds, the pace is quickening and it won't be long before their distinctive silhouettes disappear from our skylines for good.

German War Cemetery

Suffolk

**THE DEATH AT MONS OF PRIVATE JOHN PARR
is commonly held to be the first of the Great War,
but in a quiet corner of a Suffolk churchyard lie
the victims of an incident recorded two weeks
earlier – several of them German.**

The very day war was declared, the Royal Navy's HMS *Amphion* was patrolling an area of the North Sea when it came across a German vessel busy laying mines. The *Königin Luise* was a hastily converted ferry, painted in Great Eastern Railways colours in the forlorn hope of escaping detection. Unfortunately for the Germans, she was only lightly armed and, after sinking her, the crew of the *Amphion* – mindful of the Nelsonian tenet 'humility in victory' – moved in to begin pulling scores of survivors out of the water.

Turning for home in the early hours of 6 August, the *Amphion* struck one enemy mine and then another. Torn apart by the blasts, there was no question of her staying afloat and several other ships in the area steamed forward to help. Despite their efforts, 131 Royal Navy personnel lost their lives, either in the blasts or as a result of their injuries. To this had to be added an unspecified number of Germans, men who had the misfortune to be hit and sunk twice in a single night.

Not all of the bodies could be recovered, and many of those who came ashore alive at Harwich were described by a waiting reporter as looking like the victims of an explosion in a coalmine. Two days later, the first casualties were buried with full military honours at St Mary's Church Shotley, an ordinary Suffolk churchyard at that time, although it eventually came to accommodate nearly 250 servicemen. Thirteen of these were German, although few visitors now seem to notice.

The carnage on the Western Front soon dwarfed these numbers, but in August 1914 all that lay in the future, and this first naval engagement of the war was rightly regarded with horror. It seems therefore extraordinary that the story has been largely forgotten, and worth noting how at this early stage in the war it was possible to treat the enemy dead with the same care and respect as one's own.

GHQ Line

HAVING ABANDONED SUCH HUGE QUANTITIES of materiel in 1940 during the retreat from Dunkirk, and lost one in eight troops as prisoners of war, the decision was taken to base Britain's security on dozens of lines of fixed defences.

Hitler's Directive No. 16, coming on 16 July 1940, left no room for complacency: 'As England, in spite of the hopelessness of her military position, has so far shown herself unwilling to come to any compromise, I have decided to begin to prepare for, and if necessary to carry out, an invasion of England.'

Having surprised even themselves at the speed with which they had forced a French surrender, Germany's armed forces were not yet in a position to press ahead with the Führer's wishes. As the Germans drew up detailed plans for what became known as Operation Sea Lion, General Sir Edmund

Ironside, Commander-in-Chief of Britain's Home Forces, raced to complete a series of static defences designed to thwart the invasion when it came.

Aside from the need to protect many hundreds of miles of coast, the longest and most important component of these fixed barriers was the General Head Quarters, or GHQ Line, which Ironside determined was likely to be the most effective way to maintain London as the seat of power.

The idea was for a coastal 'crust' of infantry to be deployed along beaches. This would be insufficient in itself to defeat an invading force, but strong enough to hold the fort while reinforcements were mustered. Further inland would be fortified lines, essentially hundreds of miles of anti-tank traps and obstacles supported by pillboxes. With a reserve of three infantry divisions and one armoured one, it was hoped that any German advance could be slowed and contained in specified areas of the country.

At a local level, defensive cordons of ditches, tank traps and pillboxes were beginning to be thrown up like mini Maginot lines around airfields, coastal batteries and radar sites. But as part of a coordinated national plan, what Ironside termed his Operation Instruction No.3, the GHQ Line was to be far more extensive. Stretching from outside Bristol to Maidstone in Kent, running north of the military town of Aldershot and slightly south of Guildford, it looped around south-east London and, crossing the Thames Estuary, continued up through Cambridge, across the Fens and beyond the Wash.

As elsewhere (see Coquet Stop Line, page 35), even quite short stretches of the line soon displayed a diverse array of different structures, from small, brick-built pillboxes scarcely larger than a sentry box to far more substantial ones designed to accommodate Bren and anti-tank guns. Most were standard designs: the size, shape, wall-thickness and so on laid out in a series of instructions from the War Office Directorate of Fortification and Works, with the Royal Engineer offices being responsible for identifying suitable locations.

The siting of many now looks quite haphazard, and as most of them were to be manned by Home Guard volunteers, the whole arrangement seems an unlikely defence against those same troops that had crushed France so quickly and decisively. Had that army crossed the GHQ Line, Britain's downfall might have been equally swift and just as certain; but happily this was never put to the test. The first line of defence was always going to be the Royal Air Force, and then the Royal Navy. These thousands of pillboxes and miles of tank traps would have been needed only had they failed, and when it mattered most, they never did.

God's Gift

Cumberland

It is an area of stunning natural beauty, the inspiration for generations of artists, poets and writers, yet an alternative history of the Lake District is as a centre of mining and heavy industry. Mineral extraction went on for at least 5,000 years and, before its disappearance, it had a surprisingly international dimension.

Besides stone for Neolithic axes, the old counties of Cumberland and Westmorland have long been a rich source of copper, lead and iron, and even small amounts of gold and silver.

Today's beautiful fells have been quarried and mined for centuries, although the work was done on a relatively modest scale until the arrival of expert German miners in the 1560s.

In that decade it was established in law that 'all mines of gold and silver within the realm, whether they be in the lands of the queen, or of subjects, belong to the queen by prerogative, with liberty to dig and carry away the ores thereof, and with other such incidents thereto as are necessary to be used for the getting of the ore'.

This legislation sparked something of a boom in mining and had far-reaching implications, not least because copper ore often contains an admixture of gold. This meant it fell under the same terms so that many of the Germans found themselves employed by the Society of Mines Royal, a profitable concern that had a monopoly across many English and Welsh counties.

One of its most valuable concessions was the Goldscope Mine, which was situated at the foot of the northern ridge of Hindscarth. The mine had been taken over by the Crown from the 7th Earl of Northumberland and its name is often assumed to be a comment on the precious metal mined there. In fact it was chiefly a source of lead and copper, and the name is simply a corruption of the German *Gottesgab*, meaning God's Gift.

Mineral deposits in this region occur in fissures and faults caused by the upward pressure of the underlying granite. The terrain and the faults' near-verticality mean that many of the mines are, for their age, incredibly deep: miners working the God's Gift veins, for example, would each day have to climb more than 200 metres back up to the surface.

In a pre-industrial age this sort of activity posed considerable technical challenges, and as shafts were driven deeper and deeper into the mountain, it became uneconomic to pump out the water. Eventually God's Gift was forced to close – it was too expensive rather than being exhausted – but not until the late nineteenth century, or more than 300 years after the Germans had first started work.

By this time it was both cheaper and easier to import copper from abroad, and as with coal a hundred years later, mines were soon closing all over the country. For a while French metallurgists attempted to use electrolysis to liberate the last traces of valuable metals from the area's abundance of spoil heaps, but by 1914 they too were gone. The old workings were left to decay, a once-vibrant industry was lost and nature began to reassert its claim to the fells.

Hydraulic Power Company

London

Supplanting steam before being rapidly overtaken by electricity, for a few short years a network of around 180 miles of tunnels and pipes running under London provided the power for lifts, cranes, dock-gates, workshops, the Royal Opera House curtains and occasionally even Tower Bridge.

At its peak in 1904, the system linked literally thousands of hotels, factories, shops, offices and mansion blocks from Earls Court to the docks in the east. To serve them, more than seven billion litres of pressurized water circulated, running from six private pumping stations to wherever the power was needed to lift, open, close or compress – year round, both north and south of the river.

The company behind all this is long gone, but a single pumping station has survived,[10] along with much of the London Hydraulic Power Company's mind-boggling infrastructure. It is mostly underground, but manhole covers marked 'LHP' provide clues as to the routes of much of the pipework. Above ground, urban explorers might also find a small, slightly mysterious circular structure near the public entrance to the Tower of London: the brick-built portal to a unique, privately owned tunnel running under the Thames.

Originally designed to carry passengers in claustrophobic wooden cable cars, the tunnel was called the Tower Subway and closed in 1894 when the new Tower Bridge enabled the public to cross the river free of charge. Taken over by LHPC, the tunnel was then used to run hydraulic power down into south London and continued doing so until technology took another significant step forward. As customers began switching to using small, on-site electric motors, LHPC went into decline and soon had a staff of just six maintaining the redundant network.

Decades later, the whole thing was acquired by the Rothschild banking family, including the old Tower Subway, for a little over a million pounds. It sounded a lot at the time, but having shrewdly identified a potential use for its many miles of pipes, tubes and tunnels – built to exceptionally high standards, they made perfect conduits for fibre-optic cables – the network was sold on to a subsidiary of a major communications multinational. In this way something that had its origins in mid-Victorian Britain now finds itself still very much fit for purpose as part of the much-trumpeted information superhighway.

10. The pumping station at Wapping has been both a restaurant and an art gallery, but others at Bankside, Grosvenor Road in Pimlico, City Road, East India Dock and Rotherhithe have been demolished.

The Jacobite Succession

Bavaria

**THE PRESENT SOVEREIGN IS DIRECTLY DESCENDED
from William the Conqueror (the Frenchman is
the queen's twenty-second great-grandfather), but
the line of succession to the throne itself has been
far from straight, and there are those who believe
the monarchy has passed down the wrong branch
of the family tree. The throne, they say, belongs
to an unmarried eighty-two-year-old Roman
Catholic, a German called Franz.**

The idea of a House of Wittelsbach instead of the familiar
House of Windsor sounds bizarre until one follows the
senior line of descent through its thirty-odd generations
from William I to Elizabeth II. Interestingly, between 1066
and today, there are almost two dozen kings and queens,
including several iconic national figures such as Henry VIII
and Bloody Mary, who are not uninterrupted father-to-child
descendants on Elizabeth II's direct line. Few would argue
that these outliers from the Conqueror's line of descent didn't
rule legitimately, but whenever anyone but the eldest son
(or, if there is no son, daughter) of the preceding monarch
accedes to the throne – as per the right of primogeniture –
there is always the potential for dissent.

Such was the case for the would-be King Franz. The
crucial date for his possible succession was 11 December
1688, the day on which James II was deposed and went into
exile in what came to be known as the Glorious Revolution.

James was succeeded by his daughter (Protestant Mary II, ruling jointly with her husband William of Orange), rather than his eldest son, the self-styled James III. Thus the nature of the Catholic king's removal – and the ensuing succession – made dissent inevitable. It also explains why, if only in tiny and, one suspects, diminishing Jacobite circles, it has never quite gone away.

How many of those still supporting the Stuart cause would wish to see Franz on the throne is impossible to know, and he has certainly never publicly voiced an interest in unseating the queen. But for those curious about how the titular Duke of Bavaria can even be considered a claimant, the following – Britain's lost Jacobite succession – shows his genuine connection to this country's last Roman Catholic king, even if his claim to the throne is tenuous.

The list includes the names of these lost sovereigns, the ones who might have been. If only the Italian-born Bonnie Prince Charlie had succeeded in his bid to regain the throne as Charles III, and thus saved his family from decades of bitter exile and marriage to the offspring of increasingly minor European royalty.

James II	Son of Charles I. Deposed.
James III	The Old Pretender, son of the above.
Charles III	The Young Pretender, son of the above.
Henry IX	Brother of the above. Died unmarried, nominating as his heir:
Charles IV	King of Sardinia, great-grandson of Charles I.
Victor	Brother of the above. Another Italian.
Mary III	Daughter of the above. A princess of Savoy.
Franz I	Son of the above. A prince of Hungary and Bohemia.

Mary IV	Niece of the above. Married Ludwig III of Bavaria.
Rupprecht	Son of the above.
Albrecht	Son of the above.
Franz II	Son of the above.

King John's Treasure

Lincolnshire

**A BIT LIKE FAGIN AT THE END OF *OLIVER!*,
the arch-villain of the Robin Hood legend is
supposed to have waited helplessly as a fortune
in gold and precious stones disappeared beneath
the oozing slime of medieval England.**

The crown jewels weren't the only things to slip from John's grasp: Normandy and Anjou were lost during his reign (1199–1216), and under the terms of Magna Carta he surrendered powers that had been the privilege of kings for generations.

The difference, however, is that no one really expects England to resume its hold over the Angevin empire, and after 800 years would anyone wish to abandon Magna Carta? Yet rumours about lost royal treasure continue to persist among metal-detectorists living in and around the Fens.

And be sure that they are only rumours. It is true that towards the end of his reign, John took refuge in East Anglia, but documentation about what he got up to is scarce. So scarce, that is, that it is impossible to be sure what, precisely, was happening where on 12 October 1216.

We know he was in Bishop's (now King's) Lynn that day, a significant port and one where, despite his growing unpopularity, the king was generally well regarded. The plan was for his party to journey to Lincolnshire, crossing the Fens to Wisbech while the royal wardobe and regalia went by wagon across the estuary. It sounds mad now, as does separating the two, but there were tidal causeways in the region and such an expedition was hardly unprecedented.

The king spent the night at Wisbech Castle, but the wagons were never seen again. John himself was not long for the world (he died of dysentery days later at Newark) and from somewhere sprang the idea that his possessions, including the crown jewels, had mysteriously disappeared. No one reported them missing. No one claimed to have seen them disappear. No one even knew where it was supposed to have happened, except somewhere on the extensive marshes around Sutton Bridge and Walpole Cross Keys. They were simply gone.

Since then the landscape has conspired to magnify the mystery. Land reclamation schemes mean that what was the surface 700 years ago is now buried six metres under it. Similarly, what was on the coast then is often several miles inland. Even Wisbech Castle disappeared, to be replaced by a nineteenth-century villa.

As is often the case with supposed El Dorados, none

of this has prevented people searching. The detectorists know their equipment can't reach beneath all that silt, but between the two world wars an American team paid local farmers 2/6d (or 12.5p) an acre to search for clues. Even Sir Mortimer Wheeler, the Keeper of the London Museum, had a poke around, favouring an approach that used a magnetic variometer to probe down into the mud.

Most recently a team from Nottingham University has examined soil samples in the area in a bid to plot the route of any potential causeways. As with Fagin, nothing so far has come to light – not even the so-called short-cross pennies John had minted at Lynn – but after eight centuries, no one is yet ready to give up the search.

Knockers-Up

THE INDUSTRIAL REVOLUTION BROUGHT
with it many changes. For millennia farm workers and
weavers had risen with the sun, but efficient factories
required regular hours and in an age when few could
afford a clock, an entirely new trade was born.

No special skills were required to be a knocker-up, besides the habits of an early riser and the willpower to do it day after day, thereby ensuring that customers were never let down. Employed in mill towns and pit villages all over the country, and in all the big cities, many were retired workers or those deemed unfit for heavy labour.

Most walked the streets using a long pole to tap on

bedroom windows; a few combined the role with that of a lamplighter (see page 74) or a night watchman, in which case a truncheon might double-up. At least one used a pea shooter, a woman called Mary Smith who worked the streets of London's East End in the 1930s and was immortalized in a much-reproduced photograph of the period. Police constables are also known to have supplemented their pay in this way, agreeing, against regulations, to rouse those living on their beats in exchange for just a small consideration.

Needless to say, no one paid much for the service – potential customers typically had nothing to spare – but the work was straightforward, if tedious, and if sufficient numbers of householders could be found, the books could be made to balance in the end. People relied on the service, but rarely gave any thanks for it, and indeed in an early chapter of *Great Expectations* Dickens makes a point of noting the church clerk's 'very bad temper' after being knocked-up.

Lamplighters

London

IT IS A LITTLE OVER **200** YEARS AGO THAT
**Pall Mall became the first street in the country to be
lit by gas, and nearly one hundred and forty since
electricity began to replace it, initially on Holborn
Viaduct and Thames Embankment. However, nearly
1,500 working gas lamps still survive in the capital,
along with the job of lamplighter.**

Once upon a time, hundreds of men were employed to do this, but today just a handful of British Gas engineers look after appliances from Bromley-by-Bow to Richmond, and as far north as Highbury. Many of the Victorian lamps are where one would expect them to be – Buckingham Palace has sixteen, although not all of them are lit every night – and others such as those in St James's Park are easily recognizable by a little cross-bar just beneath the lamp. This is for the lamplighter to lean his narrow ladder against while he diligently tends to his task.

Tiny pilot lights mean that today the lamps are mostly self-igniting, but a clockwork mechanism inside each glass controls the flow of gas. This needs to be wound by hand every ten days, and reset twice a year when the clocks go back or forward. The lamplighters are also responsible for routine maintenance, such as cleaning the glass or replacing it when (as happens occasionally) it gets broken, and installing new mantles of silk dipped in lime oxide.

Gently illuminating Smith Square, Lord North Street and the northern approach to Tower Bridge, wherever you find these old gas lamps it is hard not to be charmed by them. They may be less effective than their modern counterparts (their power is equivalent to just forty watts), but the glow is soft and seductive, particularly against the backdrop of some of London's finest and most historic architectural set pieces.

The Last Duel

Surrey

FOR AS LONG AS MAN HAS HAD FISTS, HE HAS had duels, but when time was finally called on the habit of gentlemen killing each other in a gentlemanly fashion, an entrenched code of honour meant the practice was a long time dying.

Fists had given way to blades and then pistols, but by the nineteenth century the practice had long since been outlawed and anyone claiming victory in a duel was liable to a charge of murder. In general, the courts tended towards leniency, and in 1841 when the 7th Earl of Cardigan found himself on trial for seriously wounding a brother officer, even Queen Victoria let it be known that she wished him to escape conviction.

He did so, on the outrageously minor technicality that the court papers mistook the name of the victim, a move that did nothing to dampen the sense of outrage that the law was applied differently to those in positions of power. In fact, public opinion had long since turned against duellists and, as in America, it was to be this rather than specific laws that finally brought an end to the tradition.

The last-known duel between Englishmen took place four years after Cardigan's acquittal on the beach near Gosport: James Seton died after being shot by Henry Hawkey from fifteen paces. Once again the winner escaped conviction when the court heard how severely provoked Hawkey had been (by the dead man's behaviour towards his wife) and determined that the cause of death was not the bullet after all, but the medical treatment administered afterwards.

But even this was not quite the last of it, and it was not until October 1852 that the last fatal duel was fought on British soil. This time the protagonists were both Frenchmen: a socialist revolutionary called Emmanuel Barthelemy and fellow refugee Lt Frederic Cournet.

The precise reason for their squabble is unknown, but it is thought to have been trivial, as it was in many of these cases. For whatever reason, Barthelemy, an engineer and veteran of the 1848 Paris Uprising, demanded satisfaction and the two met at Englefield Green near Windsor.

Preferring pistols over swords, Cournet won the toss and chose his position. It was agreed that the pair would face each other from forty paces, and that neither would fire before taking ten paces forward. Each would be permitted two shots,

excluding misfires, and if both remained standing, swords would be drawn.

Cournet missed his first shot and was then hit 'with fatal precision' by his opponent after two misfires. In court Barthelemy was acquitted of murder, but found guilty of manslaughter, and sentenced to a few months in jail. His story might have ended once he had served his time, but in 1854 he was in court again. This time he was charged with murdering his employer George Moore, and shooting a neighbour who had attempted to prevent him getting away. But there was to be no escape, and the following January the last man to survive a duel in England was hanged outside Newgate Gaol.

Lindley

Leicestershire

A DOMESDAY VILLAGE THAT DISAPPEARED IN THE Middle Ages, leaving nothing but its name (to a wartime airfield), Lindley is now lost beneath the Motor Industry Research Association's more than sixty miles of sophisticated test tracks and high-speed circuits.

Almost nothing is known of the settlement on the Warwickshire–Leicestershire border, aside from its disputed claim to be the dead centre of England. One of around several thousand documented deserted medieval villages (see Gainsthorpe, page 57), it briefly lived on in the name of RAF Lindley, but as a relatively modest training and transport base, it was operational for just three years before its closure in 1946.

Initially government-funded as part of a post-war bid to improve British carmakers' competitiveness overseas, the new Motor Industry Research Association moved onto the 760-acre former airfield two years later. Three abandoned runways would let engineers test and develop new vehicles out of sight of rivals and the public, allowing them to experience speeds that would be neither safe nor sensible on normal roads.

The emphasis on new and advanced technology was underlined at the official opening ceremony when a small quantity of explosive was used to cut the tape, and a number of ex-military buildings were brought back into use, including an aircraft hangar and a control tower. As the motor industry expanded, however, so did the demands it placed on MIRA. A high-speed circuit was built, on which cars typically averaged more than 100 mph,[11] followed shortly by other specialized facilities such as the Belgian Pavé track – a mile-long stretch of cobbles designed to test what engineers call NVH or noise, vibration and harshness – and sealed chambers to simulate the extremes of heat and cold.

With much of the work today shifting towards economy, safety and the environment, MIRA continues to be an internationally important centre for many aspects of transport research. Britain may no longer own a single automotive manufacturer of any size or significance, but it builds and exports more cars than at any time in the past. Happily, the foreign companies that own the factories in which these are built, many of which have far longer histories than MIRA, continue to rely on British technical, engineering and manufacturing expertise.

---

11. On 16 December 1998, a fully road-legal McLaren F1 averaged 168 mph around the 2.82 mile circuit, reaching a maximum speed of 196.2 mph.

Lines of Communication

London

**IN 1643, THE OLD ROMAN WALL AROUND LONDON
was no longer considered sufficient defence
against the Royalist army of Charles I. Work
began on the construction of an encircling series
of ramparts, forts and magazines, although none
of this has survived.**

Commissioned by Parliament 'for the better Securing
and Safety of the said City, Suburbs, Parliament, City of
Westminster and Borough of Southwarke', the lines of
fortifications are clearly visible on a highly detailed map
produced in 1738 by George Vertue. This means it is possible
to trace the route on foot, although great imagination is
required to summon up an image of the large earthworks
and nearly two dozen defensive positions that encompassed
the capital at this stage of the Civil War.

With a population of less than 700,000, it was possible
to enclose the whole of the capital within a boundary that at
no point was more than a mile and a half from the centre.
Building work nevertheless involved an estimated 20,000
volunteers and militiamen (many thousands recruited from
the membership of the city's livery companies), and with
admirable efficiency the eighteen-mile-long barrier was
completed and ready in just a couple of months.

Beginning east of the Tower of London, the line of
defences tracked north up to the old Royal London Hospital,
crossing the modern Hackney Road and Kingsland Road

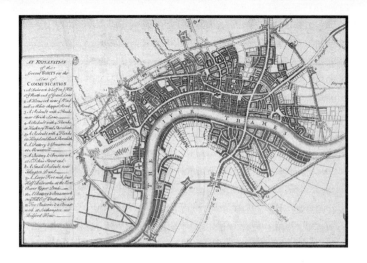

before turning south-west towards Gray's Inn. Passing through Bloomsbury and by what is now New Oxford Street, they continued on to Hyde Park Corner, Tothill Fields in Westminster and the natural barrier of the river.

Across the water at Vauxhall, a similar line ran northeast up to St George's Fields (near a late-eighteenth-century obelisk commemorating Brass Crosby's tenure as London's Lord Mayor) before turning sharply east to meet Borough High Street, Tabard Street and the Old Kent Road. A final stretch running northwards joined the Thames, terminating directly opposite our starting point on the north bank.

Detailed descriptions of the precise form of the fortifications do not exist, but the Lines of Communication are known to have incorporated forts or redoubts of different sizes, as well as a variety of ditches, batteries, bulwarks, breastworks and hornworks of the sort common during this period. Designed with the help of Dutch military engineers, the combination sounds formidable, but in the event none of this was ever put to the test. After barely four years, the lines were dismantled, so totally as to leave no physical trace of their brief existence.

Llanwddyn

Montgomeryshire

SEVENTY-FIVE INCHES A YEAR OF WELSH RAIN
has to go somewhere, and in the principality's
own Lake District, the lost village of Llanwddyn
deserves to be remembered as one of the victims
of the Victorians' civic ambition and some
hugely impressive engineering.

The names Bala, Vyrnwy, Craig Goch, Garreg-ddu and Caban Coch may not chime with quite the same resonance as Coniston, Ullswater or Windermere, but they don't attract the same crowds, either. Indeed, visiting the lakes of mid-Wales, one could be forgiven for thinking the coaches queuing to enter Cumbria's Keswick are going in the wrong direction.

The largest of the Welsh lakes, Vyrnwy, is one of the most beautiful anywhere in Europe and, ringed by mountains, lies at the centre of 23,000 acres of forest, farmland, moors and nature reserves, much of which is open to the public. Approached from the south-east, the lake itself could hardly be mistaken for a natural one, however, as the first thing one encounters is more than half a million tonnes of solid stone dam. Curiously, though, knowing the lake is the work of man and not nature makes it somehow even more remarkable.

Nearly five miles long, covering more than 1,100 acres and containing 60 billion litres of water,[12] Lake Vyrnwy is essentially a vast, drowned glacial valley. Its construction was

12. In time-honoured fashion this has been estimated as equivalent to 2,500 Olympic-size swimming pools or 604 Royal Albert Halls.

part of an 1880s scheme to supply clean fresh water to the rapidly expanding city of Liverpool nearly seventy miles away, just as Craig Goch, Garreg-ddu and Caban Coch were created to serve Birmingham.

Like them, it still fulfils this important function, and today there is little to match the experience of walking along the great dam and feeling the raw power as a biblical torrent of water spews noisily through the arches at its lofty crest.

A typically grandiose piece of Victorian urban planning, it speaks of an age when impact and aesthetics were considered central to good design. As a result, everything about Vyrnwy has the same air of invincible solidity, providing a lesson in the way in which the very best man-made structures can blend beautifully with the most glorious natural surroundings.

The picturesque straining or valve tower beneath which the water begins its forty-eight-hour journey to Liverpool may look like the sort of fairy-tale castle Mad King Ludvig of Bavaria fancied, but it is hard not to be awed by the Victorians' accomplishment and their stunning attention to detail.

Of course, all this came at a price – a heavy one in addition to the £620,000 spent on the ambitious ten-year project. Most obviously it spelt the death of the village of Llanwddyn, a long-established community at the foot of the valley whose inhabitants had to be forcibly removed and rehoused before the water levels began to rise.

Some moved to the cities, but those who remained, like the nearly 1,000 skilled masons brought in to dress blocks of stone weighing more than ten tonnes apiece, were found homes in a brand-new Llanwddyn. These were clearly better equipped than their predecessors, and better built, but it is hard to deny that something must have been lost beneath the inky-black waters, besides the old parish church, a post office, two chapels, and the intriguingly named Cross Guns Inn.

Local Time

Hertfordshire

**CLOCK TOWERS ARE NOWADAYS LITTLE MORE THAN
architectural adornments: attractive, but
expensive to maintain. Yet for centuries they
provided an essential public service when towns
ran on their own time, domestic clocks were rare
and watches unknown to all but the very rich.**

Some 2,000 years ago in Athens, the Tower of the Winds
was fitted with eight sundials and, centuries later, a 'cosmic
engine' powered by water provided visitors to Song-dynasty
China with displays of astronomical information, including
the relative position of the sun and stars.

Clocks with faces came later, however, and one of the first
in Britain was installed in a tower in the middle of St Albans.
Built between 1403 and 1412, this is the sole surviving
medieval clock tower in the country and, as such, a source of
great civic pride.

After all, time was in those days very much a local matter
and differed from town to town as one travelled east or west.
Measured by the sun, Oxford lagged a full five minutes behind
London, Leeds six, and Bristol another four behind that – all
of which would have been confusing, except that travelling
from one to the other took so many hours, or even days, that
a few minutes was neither here nor there.

Things stayed that way until the coming of the railways,
when faster travel made it necessary to devise some kind of
standardized national time. Even then, many places held out,

refusing to bow down to London[13] until the passing in 1880 of the Statutes (Definition of Time) Act enabled Parliament to force the entire country to adopt Greenwich Mean Time.

In St Albans, it won't have made much difference: with a longitude of 0.336° west, the town is very close to London. Most people probably couldn't have read a clock anyway – chiming bells were often more useful – and so the tower fulfilled other roles such as ringing the evening curfew and as a lookout for local watchmen. Later still, a shutter telegraph on the top allowed the Admiralty to send semaphore messages from London to the fleet at anchor in Great Yarmouth, taking just minutes instead of three days by horse.

Lord High Admiral of the Wash

Norfolk

ONE OF SEVERAL ANCIENT HEREDITARY POSTS that brought colour to British Isles history, since medieval times the Lord High Admiral of the Wash was charged with protecting the realm from an attack on that part of East Anglia.

Strictly speaking, he lost his job in the 1700s, when the

---

13. Many cathedrals refused to reset their clocks and some station clocks were fitted with separate minute hands showing local and London time.

responsibility for defending the coast sensibly passed to the Royal Navy. However, his descendants, the Le Strange family of Hunstanton in Norfolk,[14] continue to claim the rank, albeit without the associated perks that once extended over the foreshore as far out as the holder could throw a spear.

Happily, not all of these wonderful old posts have vanished. The Constable of the Tower of London is still able to take the contents of any carts falling into his moat and a barrel of rum from Royal Navy vessels moored at Tower Pier. Similarly, the Queen's Bargemaster continues to guard the royal regalia, even though the Crown Jewels rarely travel anywhere by boat.

But these are rare exceptions, and mostly such ancient roles have been allowed to die off rather than actually been killed off. For example, the Fellowes family maintains the right of its eldest unmarried daughter to strew sweet-smelling herbs along the path of the sovereign at a coronation, although no one has taken them up on the offer since George IV in 1820. Similarly, neither Edward VIII nor George VI, nor indeed our present queen felt the need to summon Scotland's official armour-bearer and squire of His Majesty's Body while travelling north of the border. And in 1953, the Grand Falconer (a hereditary role) was forbidden

14. One holder, Sir Roger L'Estrange (1616–1704, pictured) provided the first English translation of Aesop's *Fables* and published an early form of newspaper called the *Public Intelligencer*.

to enter Westminster Abbey unless he swapped his live bird for a stuffed one.

Today, as a result, we can only wonder if being Keeper of the Royal Firebuckets was a full-time job, or how one got to become Grand Carver of England, and whether the Clerk to the Board of Green-Cloth was being rewarded or demoted when he was appointed to the post of Embellisher of Letters to the Eastern Princes. A modern monarchy can clearly manage without them, but it's a shame that so many have gone for good.

Lost

Aberdeenshire

WITH ITS MUCH-PHOTOGRAPHED VILLAGE SIGN,
this small Upper Donside hamlet isn't so much
lost as Lost, an Anglicization of the Scots Gaelic
Lòsda.

What has been lost, however, is the aforementioned sign, so many of which have been stolen in recent years that the local council finally decided the village ought to change its name to something less appealing to light-fingered motorists.

Residents naturally objected, and the councillors eventually backed down, agreeing instead to weld the replacement sign to its posts instead of merely clipping it on, and to set the posts into larger-than-usual blocks of concrete. Their solution seems so far to have worked.

Lundenwic

London

**IT MIGHT BE ASSUMED THAT WHEN THE ROMANS
withdrew, the next wave of invaders simply
moved into the buildings they left behind
but, in fact, the location of the Anglo-Saxon's
London was lost for centuries and, even now,
their history remains mysterious.**

Roman Londinium has always been easy to find on a map. The outline of London's famous square mile is more or less that of the old walled city, and besides long stretches of wall, surviving relics from the period include a temple, the forum, an amphitheatre, bathhouse, and several floors and mosaics.

Of Lundenwic, however, almost everything is lost. At All Hallows by the Tower, the City of London's oldest church, with a foundation date of AD 675, a late seventh-century arch is not only the oldest fragment of church architecture anywhere in the capital but the sole piece of Saxon masonry found above ground.

The Saxons, in truth, were not great builders and their preference for wood over brick or stone means they left behind little more than traces of their time in London. In part this explains why it took until the 1980s for their lost settlement to be discovered about a mile west of Londinium, and why we know so little about them compared to the Romans.

At that time excavations in and around Covent Garden suggested a substantial settlement covering approximately

150 acres, stretching from what is now Trafalgar Square across to Aldwych. Over more than twenty years, finds in this area have included an early Saxon cemetery (beneath the London Transport Museum), traces of rubbish heaps and wells, an amber necklace, and some evidence that textiles, metals and glass were once made here.

The name Aldwych comes from *Ealdwic*, meaning an 'old market' or 'trading place'. This clearly chimes with the Venerable Bede's description of Lundenwic as 'a trading centre for many nations who visit it by land and sea', and it is now thought that the prefix 'old' was adopted after a move by the population to occupy the ruins of the walled Roman city when they came under attack from Vikings in the ninth century and after.

Maine Road Stadium

Manchester

DESPITE THE EXPENSE AND FREQUENT
**disappointments, controversies and corruption,
English soccer fans remain strangely loyal to the
game and rarely more so than when a historic,
much-loved stadium is threatened with demolition.**

Arsenal's Highbury ground was lucky in that its protected Grade II-listing ensured its at least partial survival when the art deco stands were converted into flats in 2006. However, many rivals have been less fortunate and around the country dozens of grandstands have been torn down and the pitches sold for redevelopment as housing or for soulless industrial or retail parks.

The example of Manchester City's Maine Road stadium is typical, the club abandoning its historic Moss Side home in 2003 and doing so in the face of strong opposition from its fans. Many of them grabbed a memento while they still could, ranging from chunks of earth ripped from the hallowed turf to battered seats sold online for little more than a few pounds to turnstiles and even toilets.

Today, houses cover most of the site, with Kippax Street marking the position of the old stand of the same name and a circular patch of grass (known as Gibson's Green after long-dead groundsman Stan Green) occupying what was the centre circle. In 2014, a time capsule was placed beneath it in the hope that it would remain sealed for 100 years.

Other grounds have similar tales to tell: after 100 years as Sunderland's ground, Roker Park has become another housing estate; so too have Derby City's Baseball Ground (1890), Millwall's Den (1910), Southampton's Dell (1898) and Middlesbrough's early twentieth-century Ayresome Park – where more than a few fans have bought houses and moved in.

A hospital now stands on what was Oxford United's Manor Ground, and a DIY store on Bristol Rovers' Eastville Stadium. Hull City's Boothferry Park has lain derelict since the club left in 2002, and Stoke City's stadium for even longer, but perhaps the unluckiest is Brighton & Hove Albion, whose Goldstone Ground was sold off before a new home for the players had even been found. That was back in 1997 and many fans have still not forgiven the owner.

Market Ouvert

London

**RECEIVING STOLEN GOODS HAS LONG BEEN A CRIME
in Britain, but until the mid-1990s it was still
entirely possible to buy them in such a fashion that
the rightful owner had no right to legal redress.**

The phrase comes from the French for 'open market' and refers to an ancient practice concerning the sale of goods of questionable provenance. Since medieval times, anything sold between sunrise and sunset at certain authorized

markets was to be considered the buyer's property, even if the seller had knowingly sold them stolen goods.

The most famous of these markets was the New Caledonian, held on the site of the old Bermondsey Abbey in south London, a place still famous for antiques but one that over the centuries earned an unsavoury reputation as a direct result of its unusual status.

Renowned for keeping peculiar hours – visiting dealers can still be seen perusing items by torchlight at 5 a.m. – its 200-odd stalls also attract the more intrepid class of tourist, many of whom afterwards cross the river to a pub in Smithfields for a full English breakfast and a 7 a.m. pint.

The idea of market ouvert is thought to have originated at a time when thieves rarely travelled and stolen goods were traded locally. If a victim of burglary couldn't be bothered to check his local market, the theory went, then that was his choice and the authorities wouldn't intervene. Today such an idea would be unworkable: it is nothing less than a thieves' charter, but it still took centuries before anyone moved to change it.

And even when they did, the motive may have been nothing more than pure self-interest: not long before the introduction of an amendment to the 1979 Sales of Goods Act, two portraits were sold at Bermondsey after being stolen from Lincoln's Inn. Signed 'Gainsborough' and 'Reynolds' and entirely genuine, they fetched just £100 apiece.

The Marsham Street Rotundas

London

WINSTON CHURCHILL WAS A GREAT
**enthusiast for the idea of waging war from
underground – while serving in the trenches he
had invented a tunnelling machine for crossing
no man's land in safety – and the 1940s saw the
creation of what was almost a secret city deep
beneath the streets of London.**

Known locally as the 'ugly sisters', and to many the
embodiment of a faceless bureaucracy, until their demolition
in 2003, Westminster's Marsham Towers were among the
country's least aesthetically pleasing. This was an irony not
lost on anyone who knew they were home to the Department
of the Environment, although even locally few realized these
1960s monsters concealed two fascinating relics of London's
wartime past.

These were the North and South Rotundas, their circular
form determined by the footprint of a pair of gasholders that
had occupied the site since 1877. When these were taken
down in the late 1930s, the government decided to utilize
their solid foundations to create twin, semi-subterranean
'citadels' for the coming war with Germany. As immense,
multi-storey air raid shelters designed to withstand a direct
hit from a 500 lb bomb, each was to have a concrete lid
almost four metres thick. One would be set aside as a reserve
should anything happen to the Cabinet War Rooms, which
formed part of a top-secret six-acre complex of offices buried

beneath Whitehall and linked to the rotundas by one of several deep-level tunnels.

Completed in 1941, the citadels were large enough to accommodate many hundreds of government officials for up to three months if necessary, and over the next few years personnel from the Air Ministry, Intelligence Department, GHQ Home Forces and Ministry of Home Security spent time here. Churchill and his wife even had bedrooms in the deepest recesses of the North Rotunda, although neither is thought to have used them.

Peace brought no change to the covert nature of the buildings. The Royal Marines guarding the complex were ordered to stand down but new, similarly clandestine, uses were found for the rotundas with the Ministry of Information moving in and installing batteries of sophisticated communications equipment. Later, a new subterranean Regional War Room was incorporated into the site – one of thirteen around the country – but this was no sooner completed than rendered redundant by the Soviets' new generation of hydrogen atomic bombs, which were more than capable of penetrating a few storeys underground.

By the 1970s, much of the space was used only for storage, and aside from two brief spells as a naval command centre (during the Falklands conflict and the first Gulf War), history seemed finally to have bypassed the rotundas. Long hidden by the office blocks built above them, with the memories of those who worked in them gradually fading, the pair were swept away in the redevelopment that followed the demolition of the Marsham Towers. Only the tunnels now remain but, like the rotundas in their day, these are never opened to the public.

Medieval Town Tram

Suffolk

**A SPECTACULAR RESTORED TRAM IN IPSWICH IS
the sole survivor of what, for its time, was
a technologically advanced solution to the
problem of moving people through the city's
medieval cityscape.**

With its handsome green and cream livery, Tramcar No. 33
is, of course, not itself medieval, merely Edwardian: it joined
the Ipswich Corporation Tramways fleet in 1904. At that
time it was a sophisticated and well-designed machine, the
interior richly wood-panelled with polished brass fittings
and its top-deck seats reversible so that no one had to travel
backwards on the return leg of a journey.

Despite having room for an impressive fifty passengers,
it was also the world's narrowest tram at just 5 feet 9 inches
(1.75 metres). This enabled two trams to pass each other in
the tightly confined thoroughfares that made up the typically
medieval streetscape of the Suffolk town, now largely swept
away by the Luftwaffe and insensitive post-war planners.

Passengers were expected to refrain from spitting and
smoking except on the top deck, although in reality most
labourers tended to walk rather than pay a fare. The trams
were popular but stayed in service only until 1926 when
Ipswich became the first town in Britain to abandon them
for electric trolleybuses (see page 159). London soldiered on
with its trams until 1952, and reintroduced a more limited
service in 2000.

Middlesex

Middlesex

IF NOT QUITE LOST, THEN CERTAINLY MISLAID, THE
**historic kingdom of the Middle Saxons exists as a
cricket club and a postal address but was swallowed
up in the 1960s, mostly by Greater London.**

In fact there are those who maintain it was the other
way round, that Middlesex swallowed London, but as
arguments go that's a pretty hard one to make stand up.

For one thing, even most people who think they live
in Middlesex would struggle to trace the outline of the
county on a map. Neither could they name the county
town, because it didn't have one. Brentford made a brief
bid for the title in 1789, but failed for lack of a town hall.
It took until 1889 to form a Middlesex County Council,
but this only met in London. The important county assizes
were similarly held in London (at the Old Bailey), the
high sheriff was appointed by the City of London, and
when Middlesex finally gained a Guildhall, this too was
in London, and has now been taken over by the Supreme
Court.

Beginning with areas such as Finsbury, Tottenham,
Kensington and Tower Hamlets, the truth is that London
had been biting chunks out of Middlesex for so long before
its final erasure that most of the functions associated with a
proper county simply never developed. The coming of the
railways only hastened this process, pulling Tottenham,
Edmonton and Enfield, Acton, Willesden, Ealing, Hornsey

and many other new suburbs closer into the city's orbit and filleting Middlesex while they did so.

In this sense the 1963 London Government Act merely formalized something that had been happening for centuries. Removing the last remaining administrative functions from a county that had served the capital and been dominated by it since the twelfth century at least, the act left no one in any doubt that Middlesex was never going to wriggle free of its grasp.

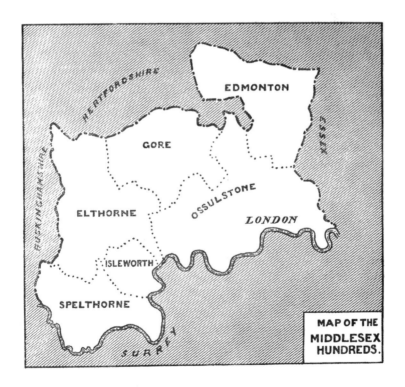

MAP OF THE MIDDLESEX HUNDREDS.

Morwellham Quay

Devon

A ONCE-POWERFUL INDUSTRY THAT TRANSFORMED the landscape of much of south-west England, the closure in 1998 of South Crofty mine brought to an end more than 3,000 years of mineral extraction in the area.

It is impossible to prove whether or not, as believers say, Joseph of Arimathea visited Cornwall's wonderfully named Ding Dong Mine to spread the word of Jesus, but the origins of mining in this area are certainly prehistoric. Tin was traditionally the most important objective (as a vital component in the production of bronze weapons), but quantities of lead, copper, manganese, zinc, arsenic and silver have also been pulled from the ground.

As well as meeting local needs, much of this natural wealth was exported. A good deal of it went to the Mediterranean and Middle East, and Greek historians such as Herodotus, Posidonius and Diodorus Siculus all wrote of the mysterious 'tin islands' in the seas beyond Gaul. To reach these overseas markets, much of the material passed through ports such as New Quay and Morwellham Quay on the River Tamar, established in the tenth century by canny Benedictine monks from Tavistock Abbey.

Britain's dominance in this field was long lived, but it declined precipitately in the late nineteenth century as new, cheaper sources of tin and copper began to emerge elsewhere in the world. Within a hundred years nothing viable remained of an industry that had dominated the landscape of Devon and Cornwall for centuries. Today both counties are littered with spoil and the ruins of old mine buildings, and honeycombed by many hundreds of collapsing tunnels and shafts.

In its heyday, Morwellham even had its own mine but, like New Quay, it mostly served others spread over a wide area. Pack animals were used to cart the metal and ore from Dartmoor and elsewhere, but with business booming to such an extent, moving goods this way was no longer practical over such challenging terrain. By 1817, the horses had been replaced by large iron barges plying the newly constructed 4.5 mile-long Tavistock Canal.

Trade peaked in the middle of that century following the discovery of huge new copper deposits – at the time the richest ever found – from the West Wheal Mary Ann mine owned by the 7th Duke of Bedford. In the mid-nineteenth century, in barely more than a month of operation, ore worth £15,300 was extracted at a cost of just £200. This sent the price of a £1 share in the mine rocketing to an astonishing £850 and required a new quay to be built at Morwellham to handle more than 30,000 tonnes annually.

It looked too good to last, and indeed it was. By 1870, the copper was mostly exhausted, and both ports were sidetracked when new railways supplanted the canals.

Almost nothing of New Quay has survived (with cruel irony its buildings were themselves 'mined', the stone stolen and sold on), and Morwellham is now an industrial heritage museum through which visitors can wander while imagining the noisy, dirty, wealth-creating organism of which it once formed a vital part.

The Motor Show

Warwickshire

BRITAIN DIDN'T INVENT THE CAR; IT NO longer owns a marque of any significance but, as a nation of petrolheads, the UK builds more cars than ever before, making it even more remarkable that it can no longer host a proper motor show.

The world's first ever motor show was organized by the scientist and author Sir David Lionel Salomons Bt.,[15] who undertook to exhibit his personal 'petroleum carriage' – an early Peugeot – at 3 p. m. on 15 October 1895 at the Agricultural Show Ground in Tunbridge Wells in Kent. More than 5,000 spectators turned up to see it (for most of them it was the first time they had ever seen such a machine), together with the Count de Dion's steam tractor, a 'one mouse-power' tricycle and a small petrol-driven fire engine.

It was, as it sounds, a modest affair, but the start of something big. Sir David is now credited with introducing the motor car to this country, and at his country house, Broomhill, he built the first motor house or garage. The idea of a motor show also took off, and for the next hundred years and more, tens of thousands of enthusiasts began packing into venues in London and Birmingham.

Keen to see the latest models, to sit in them if at all

---

15. The nephew and heir of the first Jewish Lord Mayor of London, Salomons was descended from Philip Salomons, who built the country's only roof-top synagogue (which survives at 26 Brunswick Terrace, Brighton).

possible and, latterly, to amass private hoards of new car brochures, for enthusiasts young and old, the event soon became the highlight of the motoring year. As the show moved from Crystal Palace to the National Exhibition Centre near Birmingham, via Olympia and Earls Court, the number of exhibits soared. So too did the razzmatazz surrounding them. Celebrities, VIPs and even minor royals were regularly photographed on some of the more upmarket stands; on others, girls draped themselves over bonnets until the organizers called a halt when their habit of skimping on clothes eventually reached its natural conclusion.

Unveiling female models in this way certainly pulled in the crowds, but it contributed to the sense that the show was losing its original, serious purpose. By 2008, and a final move to Excel in the London Docklands, it was obvious that most manufacturers clearly preferred Tokyo, Geneva and Frankfurt, and with more tyre-kickers and brochure collectors in attendance than customers, several big names had already pulled out.

The next two shows were cancelled, and that seemed to be that. Although at the time of writing Prince Michael of Kent is among those talking up a relaunch for 2016, few in the industry are expecting a return to the glory days.

The Mound of Down

County Down

**THE VERY NAMES DOWNPATRICK AND COUNTY DOWN
come from *dun*, meaning fortification, but for
centuries the fort in question was lost and no
one really knew where it had been.**

The loss is all the more remarkable because even in an area rich in drumlins, one might have expected one of Western Europe's largest-ever Iron Age hill forts to stand out.

Drumlins, after all (from the Irish for 'little ridge'), are glacial features, but the Mound of Down was clearly man-made, yet somehow managed to evade identification and proper study until recently.

Located in the Quoile Marshes on the outskirts of Downpatrick, the massive earthwork comprises a bank and ditch encircling an egg-shaped drumlin, effectively forming an island refuge within the marsh. Covering an area of more than three acres and enclosing another horseshoe-shaped earthwork, its maximum height of more than twelve metres would once have provided an outstanding view over the surrounding countryside and the perfect defensive position against marauding troops forced to launch their assault from a disadvantageous position low down in the wide outer ditch.

Its other name, Dundalethglas, meaning 'the English Mount', is thought to refer to its possible later use by Anglo-Norman knight Sir John de Courcy who, serving under Henry II, led the invasion of Ulster in the 1170s. De Courcy subsequently colonized much of Down and Antrim, but sometime between then and now the giant mound became overgrown and was gradually lost to memory as it disappeared from view beneath the trees, gorse and brambles.

Today, as its history begins to unfold, researchers are increasingly confident that the site could be even more significant than the de Courcy connection suggests. Some are even daring to speak of a possible royal stronghold and a link with the Dál Fiatach dynasty[16] that ruled this region as kings of Ulster during the early Christian and early medieval periods.

Mumbles Sail Railway

Glamorgan

**JAPAN ONCE RAN BUSES FUELLED BY WOOD,
Rover built a jet car so temperamental that only
unmarried volunteers were allowed to test it,
and the French tried compressed air to power
aircraft and submarines.**

The prize for the most bizarre form of alternative power goes to the Welsh, however, and their unique attempts to use wind on what is fondly remembered as the world's first ever passenger railway.

The Mumbles or Oystermouth Railway was originally built to carry newly quarried limestone and iron ore into Swansea, but on 25 March 1807 the first ever fare-paying passengers clambered on board and history was made. The

16. Members were later known as the Mac an Ultaigh (Son of the Ulstermen), a name which has latterly been anglicized as MacNulty.

idea for this came from local entrepreneur Benjamin French, who paid the railway owners twenty pounds for the right to conduct a twelve-month experimental service.

In those days the single carriage was pulled by a horse, but it ran on primitive rails beginning at a station known as the Mount. (Another world first, this stood roughly where Swansea Museum is today.) Contemporary illustrations suggest a lofty and somewhat top-heavy arrangement, with four large wheels, wide running boards and seating inside and on top for at least a dozen passengers. The driver sat high up at the front in the manner of a stagecoach driver and the route was approximately five miles long.

Even not quite full, it looks a heavy load for a single horse, and so it proved, prompting a number of modifications, which, in the first instance, involved fitting it with a sail to reduce the strain on the animal. Unsurprisingly, the initiative failed almost immediately. As soon as the wind changed direction, any slight benefit was nullified and then reversed, with the sail acting as a giant air-brake whenever the wind came from any direction but perfectly astern.

The failure didn't kill the service, but a new road did when one was built around Swansea Bay not long afterwards. Anyone wishing to visit the pretty little fishing village of Oystermouth could now do so whenever they wished, saving themselves a shilling fare (5p), and by travelling on foot probably beating the time set by the horse.

The railway itself, nevertheless, survived, but only by reverting to hauling goods rather than people. In the 1870s a steam train was introduced to the line (initially, crazily, this was expected to share the single track with the old horse-drawn service) and, carrying passengers once again, the line was subsequently converted to battery power before the introduction of petrol and then diesel locomotives.

When electric trams replaced the latter in 1929, the railway claimed another world first as the first service anywhere to have tried no fewer than seven different forms of motive power.

In its final iteration, as a tramway, it was a great success, and by surviving the best efforts of Second World War German air crews, the bright-scarlet trams soon became a cheerful symbol of a defiant Swansea. After the war they were carrying more than five million trippers a year, but once again there were soon moves afoot to kill off the service.

This time the threat came from buses or, more accurately, the bus company that had taken ownership of the line. Despite healthy passenger numbers and a popular and lively campaign to keep the railway running, on 5 January 1960 the last tram left its shed for the last time. Astonishingly, no one in authority seemed prepared to recognize the railway's unique status (the Royal Institution of South Wales Museum publicly expressed 'no historical interest' in preserving even a single tram), and within hours of its closure the rails were torn up and melted down for scrap.

The Munitionettes' Cup

North Yorkshire

AMID TALK OF WOMEN'S FOOTBALL ENTERING A golden age, few supporters or players appreciate that the sport's real heyday was a hundred years ago – and that at its peak it was suddenly banned.

It was during the Great War that the game really got into its stride, when as many as 50,000 spectators would pay to see all-female sides. Clearly the women were filling a gap while the professionals were away fighting but, equally, they were doing it every bit as well as when they stepped up to the challenge of replacing the hundreds of thousands of male factory workers who went to fight overseas.

From the start their matches proved immensely popular and made stars of many of the players. Women such as Lily Parr, a six-footer who scored more than 1,000 goals during the course of her career; Jennie Morgan, who left her own wedding early so as not to miss a match; and Bella Raey, whose hat-trick gave her team victory in the 1917 Munitionettes' Cup Final.

As the championship's slightly patronizing name suggests, the games involved teams drawn from munitions factories. At one time, almost a million women made up approximately 80 per cent of the workforce in the vital armaments industry, working to great effect although typically receiving half the wage payable to men in similar employment.

What began as informal kickabouts rapidly evolved into more formalized games, and with factory managers keen to maintain a fit and physical workforce, a league was soon established. Many factories formed their own teams and matches were frequently played (occasionally against recuperating soldiers) to raise money for war charities and the like.

The all-women matches proved easily the most popular, however, even though expert opinion had always been that women were biologically unsuited to the game. Fortunately, no one had explained this to the members of Preston's Dick, Kerr's Ladies FC, nor to those playing for Blyth Spartans, nor indeed to their supporters, who began attending matches in record-breaking numbers.

It was Blyth Spartans that won the inaugural Munitionettes' Cup at Middlesbrough – beating Bolckow Vaughan 5–0, thanks to the aforementioned hat-trick – but the real victory went to Dick, Kerr's Ladies, who kept on playing after the war. In 1920 it was their team that attracted the largest ever crowd – 53,000 in the stadium, with another 14,000 congregating outside to hear the result – and with it the spiteful disapproval of the sport's governing body.

Suddenly, self-styled experts were popping up to warn of the dangers the women were subjecting themselves to, and in Harley Street in London, Dr Mary Scharlieb gleefully added football to contraception and divorce and everything else she felt working-class women should have nothing to do with. It was, she said, 'most unsuitable, too much for a woman's physical frame'.

Unsurprisingly, her arguments cut little ice with players or fans and so, a few months later, the Football Association formally advised its members not to allow women onto their pitches. The ban was an immediate and fatal blow to the sport. It remained in place for the next fifty years, doing irreparable damage to the women's game, as had been the FA's sole intention all along.

Norn

Shetland and Orkney

A TRUE LANGUAGE RATHER THAN AN ACCENT OR **dialect, Norn was spoken in Scotland's Northern Isles from the ninth century onwards, but died out some time in the mid-nineteenth century.**

Derived from the Norse tongue spoken in coastal communities in southern Norway, Norn arrived in Shetland with settlers travelling west towards Iceland and the Faroes. It is impossible to know the extent to which the language was dominant in the islands over the course of a thousand years, and indeed it may already have been in retreat by the fourteenth century when Shetland and Orkney came under Scottish control.

For a while both island groups were almost certainly bilingual, but with new Scottish overlords the Scots language would have been seen as the more prestigious of the two, being the language of choice among the ruling elite. From the 1400s Norn may have been restricted to the lower orders, the crofters and fishermen who made up the bulk of the (admittedly sparse) population, and those living in the even more isolated communities of Unst in the far north and Foula.

Today it is popularly supposed that the last native speaker was one Walter Sutherland, an inhabitant of Skaw near Haroldswick on Unst. Little is known about him besides his death around 1850 in what is reputed to have been the most northerly house in the British Isles.

Unfortunately, the paucity of written texts means that the

language is unlikely to enjoy a revival, although Norn and the other languages classified as West Scandinavian are still studied by academics. For the rest of us, Norn's flavour can be gauged from the following, a surviving fragment of the traditional Lord's Prayer, parts of which will be recognizable even to those who speak only English.

> *Fyvor or er i Chimeri.*
> *Halaght vara nam dit.*
> *La Konungdum din cumma.*
> *La vill din vera guerde*
> *i vrildin sindaeri chimeri.*
> *Gav vus dagh u dagloght brau.*
> *Forgive sindorwara*
> *sin vi forgiva gem ao sinda gainst wus.*
> *Lia wus ikè o vera tempa,*
> *but delivra wus fro adlu idlu.*
> *For do i ir Kongungdum, u puri, u glori.*

Noviomagus

Kent

AS HAPPENED IN LONDON, YORK AND COLCHESTER, it is not uncommon for Roman towns to disappear beneath new ones. Others simply get lost, however, only surviving as a few tantalizing clues in ancient documents and continuing to evade the efforts of those most determined to find them.

Noviomagus is one such example, a trading town that is mentioned in several contemporary accounts of life in Roman Britain, but whose whereabouts have continued to elude searchers on the ground. Admittedly, a few nineteenth-century antiquarians were inclined to accept a theory proposed by an Irishman, Thomas Crofton Croker, who formed a drinking club called the Society of Noviomagus after deciding the lost town was probably somewhere near Bromley.

Another theory pointed to Croydon but, here too, there was no real physical evidence and, once again, the town was presumed lost. Chronicles such as the possibly third-century Antonine Itinerary mentioned it several times, but mostly the writer was annoyingly vague. The best of them pointed to a position somewhere south of London, but said little

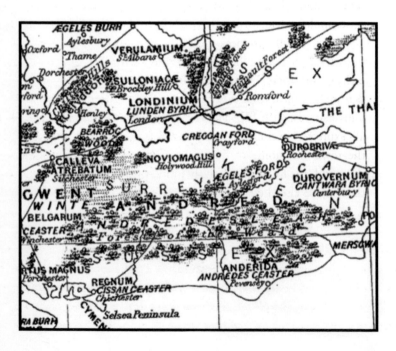

more than that a traveller would pass through it at some point on his journey from Hadrian's Wall to the south coast – a distance of more than 400 miles.

It took until 2000 before someone had another stab at identifying the town. This time it was an archaeologist from Kent, Brian Philp, who went public only after spending more than thirty years discreetly digging around for evidence to support his long-held idea that Noviomagus might be somewhere near West Wickham.

Understandably, he was keen to avoid attracting treasure hunters to the site, although what has come to light is far from the usual definition of treasure. Mostly his discoveries have been pieces of glass from Gaul and Germany pottery, along with scraps of timber and faint traces of buildings. In other words, the kind of things that thrill archaeologists rather more than they do the nighthawkers and other unscrupulous detectorists.

Since 2000, modest finds have continued to be unearthed (including the rim of a Roman wheel, a particular rarity), but there is still nothing substantial enough to definitely confirm that this is the spot. Experts from Oxford University, English Heritage and the British Museum have all expressed excitement at the idea but if, as supposed, the town was home to 500 people, maybe as many as a thousand, the finds are relatively modest when compared to those made elsewhere in Roman Britain.

Old Money

£.s.d.

**THE TRADITIONAL POUND, SHILLING AND PENNY HAD
their origins in the Romans' *librum, solidus* and
denarius, but there was nevertheless something
solid and deliciously British about old money
before its undemocratic and slightly sinister
abolition in February 1971.**

Few people realize it now, but the public didn't ask for
decimalization. Voters weren't even consulted about whether
or not it was a good idea, back in the 1960s when Labour's
Harold Wilson was casting around for a way to demonstrate
how progressive and modern he was compared to tweedy old
Tories like Harold Macmillan and Alec Douglas-Home.

In fact there was nothing remotely new about decimal
currency. Russia had introduced it nearly 200 years previously,
French revolutionaries saw it as the perfect symbol of their
determination to break with the hated Ancien Régime, and
Napoleon Bonaparte took it with him as his murderous armies
rampaged around Europe.

Wilson too saw it as a useful symbol, part of a bid to forge
a new Britain in what he called the 'white heat' of the scientific
and technological revolution. Unfortunately, the latter was seen
in the cancellation of several major aerospace projects, thereby
eviscerating the aviation industry; the gross inefficiencies of a
re-nationalized steel industry; and pressure being brought to
bear on carmakers to create a single, unwieldy behemoth –
British Leyland – about which no more needs to be said.

No one supposed that going decimal could undo such damage, but it might send out a modernizing message and show Charles de Gaulle and others in the Common Market how keen Britain was to follow the European example. After a twenty-second exchange between Wilson and his Chancellor of the Exchequer, the idea was put to the Cabinet, and with barely a murmur the ha'penny, thrupenny bit, tanner, bob, florin and half-crown were sent for scrap.

Their replacements are probably easier to understand, and having a hundred pennies in the pound instead of 240 sounds straightforward. But the old system had been around for centuries, and ditching it cost the country a fortune – at least £4 billion in today's terms – as well as alarming shoppers that the changeover would give retailers a chance to up their prices.

Forty years on, many still worry that the change was the first real chip away at the block of Britain's independence, the start of a long process of unwelcome Europeanization that no one voted for. Sensing the beginning of the end of centuries of proud island insularity, it is hard not to think the UK may have lost something more than just her money.

Old Sarum

Wiltshire

IT IS EASY TO SEE HOW AN OLDER SETTLEMENT might eventually get lost beneath a much newer one, but at Old Sarum almost the opposite has happened.

On a hill around two miles from Salisbury, buried beneath one of the most significant Iron Age sites in Europe, an entire medieval city has somehow disappeared. Dating back to 400 BC, the huge oval complex began as an important prehistoric fort before being occupied by Romans and then Saxons, who turned it into a defensive position against Viking marauders.

Later still, the Normans built a traditional round motte and bailey on the highest point of the hill. Then, during the Plantagenet reign (Eleanor of Aquitaine was held prisoner in the castle during this period), an important stone-walled city developed around it, complete with royal palace, cathedral and two large residential areas. Archaeological evidence of furnaces and kilns within the earthworks also indicates that Old Sarum was a thriving industrial centre.

It was Pope Honorius III in the early thirteenth century who signed the city's death warrant when he agreed that the cathedral community could move to a new site at New Sarum, in what is now Salisbury. Building work began in April 1220 and when the existing cathedral was dissolved six years later, much of the population had already vacated their homes. The process accelerated as Old Sarum was ransacked to provide materials for New Sarum, and when Edward II had the castle dismantled in 1322, almost nothing and no one was left.

Or so it seemed until archaeology students from the University of Southampton began surveying the site in the summer of 2014. Now, without a single sod being dug, the magic of geophysics and ground-penetrating radar has enabled the entire city to be mapped down to the level of individual buildings. In a very real sense the old city of Old Sarum is lost, but at least we know where it was.

The Opperman Stirling

Hertfordshire

**REPRESENTATIVE OF AN ENTIRE CLASS OF MOTOR
vehicle, this small but smartly styled coupé
was deliberately killed off by much bigger boys
fearful of a little competition.**

In the 1950s, when Chairman Leonard Lord gave the green
light to plans for a ground-breaking new car, he left no one
at the British Motor Corporation in any doubt as to his
intentions. 'Goddamn these bloody awful bubble cars,' he told
anyone who would listen. 'We must drive them off the road by
designing a proper miniature car.'

The car he wanted to build was the Mini, an authentic
automotive icon, although his company famously lost money
on every one it sold. The object of his ire was the increasingly
successful micro-car industry, which (beginning in post-war
Germany, where a shortage of materials dictated designs that
were cheap to build and run) was spreading across Europe in
the wake of the 1956 Suez Crisis and a hike in petrol prices.

Some micro-cars were indeed pretty awful, and a few such
as the Heinkel and Isetta displayed an undeniable bubble-like
quality. But others were handsome and often quite ingenious
in the way they squeezed the most out of the concept of cheap
motoring. Today the best are highly sought after, with some
Messerschmitts and Goggomobils attracting six-figure bids
when, very infrequently, they come up for auction.

But even these rarities are common compared to the
Opperman Stirling, which first appeared in 1958 before

disappearing just months later. In theory, customers were offered a choice of two engines, 424 or 493cc but, in practice, thanks to the bigger Lord and Co., they weren't being offered anything at all.

At its debut at the 1958 Motor Show (see page 100), what might have been this country's best-ever micro-car aroused plenty of interest from would-be buyers, but sadly no one got to take it for a test drive. With component suppliers warned off having anything to do with Opperman for fear of upsetting the irascible, bullying Lord, the Elstree-based factory managed to build just two prototypes before shutting up shop.

The tragedy was that then – just as now – small cars made a lot of sense. Unfortunately, larger cars make larger profits, which is why the industry still spends all its time and effort persuading customers to spend money they haven't got on cars they can't afford to impress people they don't know.

Orford Ness

Suffolk

FOR EIGHTY YEARS A TOP-SECRET MILITARY RESEARCH base that was strictly off-limits to the public, this gloriously desolate wasteland is dotted with some of Britain's strangest and most enigmatic ruins.

At nearly ten miles long, Europe's most extensive vegetated shingle spit deserves to be world-famous and probably would be had the military authorities not succeeded in shutting off the entire area for almost the whole of the twentieth century.

Today it is a uniquely fragile natural habitat of international importance, but for decades Orford Ness was as busy and buzzing as any other military base in Britain, although villagers on the mainland could only guess at what was going on just a few hundred metres offshore.

Beginning before the First World War, it was here on the Ness that hugely significant advances were made in aerial bombardment, in military radar and communications, and in a vital part of Britain's independent nuclear deterrent, once the facilities had been reorganized as an outpost of the Atomic Weapons Research Establishment.

It could not be more different now. Reached by boat from the little harbour at Orford, the vast plain of pebbles, sea pea and saltmarsh plants instead attracts birders and naturalists, as well as military historians and others keen to explore the extraordinary ruined 'pagodas'. These were built to test nuclear weapon components during the Cold War, their strange shape designed to absorb the blast and minimize the impact of any accidental explosions.

Lying on the floor in one anonymous-looking hut is a frightening relic from the period, a genuine WE177A atomic bomb, which, in 1969, gave the Royal Navy's Fleet Air Arm the ability to drop a load equivalent to 10,000 tonnes of TNT. Other buildings, many now skeletal and quite spooky, were used to pioneer advances in parachute design, aerial photography, bomb, and gun ranging and even the development of camouflage.

Thousands were employed here over the years, including several German POWs who were buried in Orford after falling victim to the 1918 Spanish flu epidemic. But now no one is left and this remote and lonely landscape is gradually returning to nature.

'Paying on the Nail'

Bristol

**A FAMILIAR EXPRESSION THAT HAS ITS ORIGINS IN A
wholly laudable practice that has been lost in the
race for business efficiency and higher profits.**

We all know what the phrase means – paying for goods or
a service without delay – but how many buyers or sellers
appreciate that, once upon a time, money actually was paid
out 'on the nail'?

The nails in this case were pillars, commonly of bronze
or cast iron and found outside trading places such as Bristol's
Corn Exchange and the city stock exchanges in Liverpool
and Limerick in southern Ireland.

In truth, no one can be sure whether the pillars were
installed as a consequence of the phrase or whether the
phrase was used to describe the way local merchants would
agree a deal and expect buyers to lay the cash out 'on the
nail' before taking the goods.

Either way, the practice is certainly ancient. The oldest
of Bristol's pillars is thought to date to the sixteenth century
and there are several places where the phrase is used in early
English literature. The oldest is thought to be in Thomas
Nashe's *Have with you to Saffron-Walden* (1596), in which a
character is recorded as saying: 'Tell me, have you a minde
to anie thing in the Doctors Booke! speake the word, and I
will help you to it upon the naile.'

Thirty years later, a member of the cast of *The City
Madam*, a play by Philip Massinger, describes 'a payment on

the nail for a manor late purchased by my master'. Several European languages, including Dutch, French and German, have similar expressions, although their use of words such as 'ongle' and 'nagel' may be derived from the Latin *ungula*, meaning claw rather than nail, and suggesting payment was simply made into the hand.

Whatever the true meaning, paying on time was surely the most honourable way to transact any kind of business but, as already noted, it is now very much a thing of the past.

Phyllis and Ada

London

BURIED ALIVE SOMEWHERE JUST BEYOND THE boundary of London's historic square mile, Phyllis and Ada became the unwitting victims of Europe's largest construction project.

The pair are two gigantic tunnel-boring machines or TBMs, part of the ambitious Crossrail scheme, which in a few years will be carrying an estimated 200 million passengers a year along rail lines running east to west through London and its environs.

The plan to drill twenty-six miles of new tunnels through London was hatched as long ago as the 1940s, but then quickly shelved when financial and other considerations conspired to exclude it from London's post-war reconstruction. By 1974 the cost had risen to £300 million, a frightening sum at the time but one that now looks like a giveaway alongside today's near-£15 billion invoice for completing what is essentially the same task.

Employing more than 8,000 people full-time, recruiting fifty companies to assist its building and as many as 50,000 contractors during the ten years of its construction, Crossrail nevertheless depended on eight of these vast machines. The aforenamed Phyllis was the first to begin work, making her slow subterranean passage from Royal Oak to Farringdon.

Nearly 150 metres long, just over seven metres in diameter and 1,000 tonnes in weight, she and her seven sisters might more accurately be described as mobile factories than mere machines. Behind immense cutting heads moving at between one and three revolutions per minute, each one carries with it all the electrical and mechanical equipment needed to inch forward at nearly 0.00037 miles per hour.[17] Grinding away forty metres beneath street level, and supervised by a twenty-man gang, onboard kitchens, canteens and toilets mean the machines can be kept working twenty-four hours a day, seven days a week.

This is all a far cry from the early tunnelling shields used by the builders of London's Tube network, but the principle is much the same. The shields depended on Sir Marc Brunel's observations of the ingenious way in which the common shipworm *Teredo navalis* keeps from being crushed as it chews its way through a wooden vessel's hull.

Where those early shields simply protected the navvies, however, as they dug through plague pits and worse, these ultra-modern TBMs do all the heavy work as well as propel themselves forward. Together they have been responsible not only for boring the tunnels but also for removing millions of tonnes of spoil, uncovering more than 3,000 plague-era skeletons from one site

17. The speed sounds glacial, but is marginally faster than an English garden snail.

alone, and installing a quarter of a million concrete liner panels.

Unsurprisingly, they are enormously expensive at around £10 million apiece, although even at this price they are considered expendable. Some 4.5 million tonnes of earth were carefully removed from the tunnels and reused – mostly to create a new nature reserve in the Essex marshes – but no plans were made to rescue Phyllis and Ada. Instead, the pair – named after the computer pioneer Phyllis Pearson and Ada Lovelace, who devised the *A to Z* – were left with no choice but to dig their own graves. Today, their work done, they lie silent and forgotten in two vast concrete tombs somewhere deep beneath Charterhouse Square.

The Pneumatic Railway

Middlesex

SOMEWHAT FASTER THAN PHYLLIS AND ADA, BUT FAR less reliable than that doughty duo, the concept of the atmospheric railway represented a daring attempt at something new and exciting, but after meeting its Waterloo it rapidly disappeared.

In 1839, a Manchester gas engineer named Samuel Clegg began working with two marine engineers called Jack and Joseph d'Aguilar Samuda. The brothers were seeking a patent for what they termed 'the adaptation of atmospheric pressure to the purposes of Locomotion on Railways'.

By June the following year they were ready to test out their theories at Wormwood Scrubs to the west of London.

On an area of land leased by the War Office to exercise cavalry horses, the brothers installed a set of conventional rails between which they laid a long pneumatic tube. This was connected to the train above by way of a piston inserted into the tube through a narrow, sealable slot.

The idea was to use a stationary sixteen-horsepower pumping engine to expel air from the tube, thereby creating a vacuum ahead of the piston. With air admitted to the rear of the tube, it was hoped that ordinary atmospheric pressure would be sufficient to drive the piston forward along with the attached train carriage. It sounded good in theory, but putting it into practice threw up numerous technical challenges, particularly when it came to preventing air leaking from the tube.

Confident that these could be overcome, Clegg and the Samudas were contracted to build a larger version for the London & Croydon Railway. Intended to run between London Bridge and Epsom, it began limited operations in

January 1846 but was forced to shut just months later, before much of the line had even been completed.

Fast running out of money, the Samudas had been unable to resolve the difficulties with leaking seals and unreliable pumps, a failure Clegg took so seriously that he more or less withdrew from public life. But other engineers still had faith in the concept, among them Isambard Kingdom Brunel, who tried a similar system on the South Devon Railway.

Sadly, he too failed – possibly because rats kept chewing through his leather seals[18] – and like the Samuda brothers before him, he eventually turned his attention to other projects, leaving the pneumatic railway idea to die a death.

Polari

London

A LOST FORM OF SLANG, ONCE POPULAR WITH STAGE actors and circus performers, the odd word still surfaces occasionally but, despite its long history, most people today have never heard of Polari, let alone heard it spoken.

From the Italian *parlare*, meaning to talk, it is thought to have arrived in this country in the seventeenth century. It did so by way of early Punch and Judy performers, such as Pietro

---

18. They were attracted by the various sealants used: combinations of beeswax, whale oil and tallow. Rival systems used bearskin, India rubber, impregnated cloth and mysterious sounding 'glands', but none to any greater effect.

Gimonde or 'Signor Bologna', who traced his craft back to the traditions of *commedia dell'arte* and was mentioned in the diary of Samuel Pepys.

By the nineteenth century, Polari had developed into a rich if slightly random mix of Italian, rhyming and backslang, cockney and even Yiddish phrases as it spread among gay performers as a sort of secret code. At a time when homosexuality was illegal, it was used to disguise the content of a conversation from eavesdroppers; at the same time its colour and variety appealed to speakers wishing to assert or emphasize a certain over-the-top campness.

Both these aspects can be detected in the characters of Julian and Sandy, the outrageous pairing of Kenneth Williams and Hugh Paddick in the *Round the Horn* radio series broadcast by the BBC in the 1960s. Half a century ago, Polari's vocabulary was still expanding, using terms adopted from the new drug culture, but its appearance in the mainstream – it also popped up in an episode of *Doctor Who* – immediately rendered it useless as a secret code.

Now largely redundant, its usage today is ironic and too knowing to count as street slang, and hip-hop and indie artists have been known to occasionally slip a word or phrase into their lyrics. Inevitably there is even an app for neophytes keen to brush up their vocab, but as a genuine means of communication, Polari has had its day.

Presentation at Court

London

THE NEWSPAPERS STILL ROUTINELY DESCRIBE
attractive middle and upper-class girls as debs or
debutantes, but the term now has little meaning
and hasn't been relevant for decades.

In 1958, the queen decided to end the custom of young
women who were well born, or wished to be seen as such,
being presented at court. Attendance had always been by
invitation only, although helpfully an invitation could be
applied for on the girl's behalf by anyone who had herself

already been presented. The sole qualification for inclusion was that girls had to be of marriageable age, and Prince Philip wasn't the only one who thought the whole thing 'bloody daft'.

The occasion marked the formal beginning of the social season. After receiving a summons to attend from the Lord Chamberlain, debs would attend in white evening gowns, even though the ceremony started at 10 a.m. Long white gloves were also de rigueur, together with pearls or family jewels, and after being presented to the sovereign, each girl would curtsey before withdrawing backwards. (Somehow the idea got around that they curtseyed to a cake, but this was never the case.)

The arrangement was harmless enough, but increasingly pointless in a world where young people were clearly able to find themselves partners without the intervention of their mothers and their mothers' friends. Its abolition nevertheless caused a certain amount of anguish among those denied their own turn in a white dress, and for a while an attempt was made to privatize the process by hosting commercial balls at which girls could meet boys and fall in love. Everyone could pretend it was just like the good old days, but without the queen it was just that – a pretence.

Project M-N

West Sussex

**AMONG THE MORE BIZARRE OF BRITAIN'S GREAT
War defences was a scheme to prevent German
submarines entering the Straits of Dover by
installing a vast underwater net stretching from
one side of the English Channel to the other.**

The Admiralty envisaged a series of twelve immense towers standing in a line on the seabed from Folkestone to Cap Gris Nez in northern France. These would provide anchorage points for the nets as well as mounting positions for heavy guns, searchlights and look-out posts. The task of constructing them fell to Guy Maunsell, a former Royal Engineers officer who had already served on the Western Front and later went on to design the extraordinary Thames Estuary forts-on-stilts that bear his name.

More than fifty metres high, each tower was to accommodate up to a hundred naval personnel, and work on the first two began in June 1918 near Shoreham Harbour.

Consuming a thousand tonnes of steel and mounted on hollow concrete bases, each tower was expected to cost around £1 million, a staggering sum at the time. With 3,000 people building them, it was impossible to conceal what was going on from people living in the area, although few, if any, guessed what the plan involved, and locally the rapidly growing structures became known only as the Shoreham Mystery.

By October, the first tower was nearly finished, but after more than four years of death and destruction across Europe, so, at last, was the Great War. In early November, Germany capitulated and work on Project M-N was immediately halted. It was decided to dismantle the second tower – so nething that took nine months, considerably longer than it had taken to build – and to find a new use for its twin.

Naturally, at this point no one knew another war was in the offing – the nets and towers might well have proved useful against the coming U-boat menace. Instead, Tower 1 was towed out of the harbour and across more than forty miles of choppy water to Nab Rock off the Isle of Wight. Once in place, stopcocks were opened allowing hundreds of thousands of litres of seawater to flood into the hollow concrete cells at its base. Once these were full, Tower 1 sank majestically to the seafloor.

Fantastically, it is still there today and is known as the Nab Rock Lighthouse. Now solar-powered and fully automated, it is the sole remaining relic of one of the Admiralty's biggest ever secrets – and a fascinating reminder of an abandoned scheme of towering ambition.

The Queen's Champion

Lincolnshire

FOR NEARLY NINE CENTURIES, A FAMILY WAS CALLED upon to provide a knight armed and 'ready in person' to do battle with anyone challenging the legitimacy of each new sovereign on the day of the coronation.

For most of the time the right to be that knight was vested

in the Dymoke family of Scrivelsby in Lincolnshire, descendants of a thirteenth-century nobleman called Robert Marmion, who himself claimed descent from the first official champion of the Dukes of Normandy.

Once settled in England, the most famous of those dukes, William the Conqueror, granted the manor of Scrivelsby to the Marmions in return for which they were required to send a champion to Westminster at each coronation. Mounted and in full armour, his duty was to defend the sovereign's honour should anyone challenge his or her right to the throne. In the event that he fought and won, the rules allowed for the champion to be rewarded with a suit of armour and the monarch's second-best horse.

Over hundreds of years, this evolved into an enjoyable piece of theatre and instead of waiting for someone to issue a challenge, the Garter Principal King of Arms would issue one of his own: 'If any person, of whatever degree soever, high or low, shall deny or gainsay our Sovereign . . . here is his Champion, who saith that he lieth, and is a false traitor, being ready in person to combat with him, and in this quarrel will adventure his life against him on what day soever he shall be appointed.'

It is not thought that anyone ever responded to the challenge, however, and the decision not to hold a coronation banquet at all for William IV in 1831 left the champion at that time somewhat high and dry. In 1902, following the accession of Edward VII, a Dymoke decided to press his claim. After consideration, his right to be in attendance on the sovereign was duly upheld but on the understanding that from then on he and his descendants would appear at each coronation as the standard bearer of England rather than suited, spurred and ready for a fight. In this way it has been possible to honour the family for their centuries of loyal service (at the time of writing the holder is a retired lieutenant colonel, the 33rd Lord of the Manor of Scrivelsby), despite a colourful tradition having passed into history.

RAF Skaw

Shetland

RUINED BLOCKHOUSES AND SINISTER CONCRETE bunkers are all that remain of a crucial island outpost of an extensive early warning radar network dating back to the early days of the Second World War.

Operationally part of the Royal Air Force, the Chain Home network was designed to track hostile aircraft approaching Britain from the north, south or east. Forming an important part of the Dowding System (named after the Battle of Britain commander of that name), it is remembered now as the first ever fully integrated air defence network.

'A most elaborate instrument of war,' Churchill called it, 'the like of which existed nowhere in the world.' Powerful enough to detect enemy aircraft massing over France, its dedicated private telephone system enabled defence chiefs to direct interceptor aircraft to wherever they were most needed and to alert anti-aircraft batteries anywhere in the country of the need to prepare for imminent action.

RAF Skaw was one of dozens of Chain Home stations, this particular one constructed close to the most northerly settlement in the UK (see Norn, page 108). Personnel here worked closely with the nearby Coastal Command flying boat base at Sullom Voe, sending British and Norwegian aircrews to patrol the North Sea, Norwegian Sea and North Atlantic, looking for German U-boats.

This was the very first place in Britain to be bombed during the war, on 13 November 1939, when four explosions were said to have claimed the lives of two rabbits. But, joking apart, before its closure in 1947, RAF Skaw's proximity to occupied Norway meant that this part of Unst was a very busy place. Such a thing is almost impossible to imagine now, in an area where even rabbits are scarce and where the only sounds are seabirds and a bitter wind whistling through the ruins.

A Railway for the Dead

Surrey

**IN ITS DAY THE WORLD'S LARGEST CEMETERY,
for nearly ninety years Brookwood in Surrey was
linked to the capital by a train service expressly
designed for carrying corpses.**

Called the London Necropolitan Railway, it ran mostly on existing rails but had three stations of its own. The façade of one is still visible on Westminster Bridge Road in central London, and there were two more in the cemetery itself: one for Anglicans and the other for religious non-conformists. This being Victorian Britain, coffins could travel first, second or third class and special hearse vans were designed

to ensure that the dead from different social backgrounds did not accidentally mingle.

Until the railway was badly damaged by German bombs in 1941, it carried between three and four dozen cadavers a week, meaning it had transported around 200,000 in its time. Such numbers sound impressive, but they were well down on expectations that, at one point, ran as high as 140 bodies a day. The 500-acre cemetery was said by its owners to be so large that it could take all of London's dead for several centuries, but having failed to secure the hoped-for monopoly, shareholders gradually lost interest.

The cemetery nevertheless survived and is now run by Woking Council, but rebuilding the railway after the Second World War proved too expensive and, aside from the façade near Waterloo, almost nothing of it has survived.

Rattray

Aberdeenshire

Rattray is a clan and a whisky but, after 5,000 years of more or less continuous occupation, the royal burgh of that name was lost almost overnight in a mighty storm.

In an area renowned for its dramatic wind-sculpted dunes, all that remains is the picturesque ruined chapel of St Mary. Even the castle has gone, one of the 'nine castles of the knuckle' – Dundarg, Pitsligo, Pitullie, Kinnaird, Wine Tower, Cairnbulg, Inverallochy, Lonmay and Rattray – which once defended the wild and rocky headland between the Moray Firth and the North Sea. Four were owned by the Comyn family, holders of high office in the medieval kingdom of Scotland, and the thirteenth-century St Mary's, one of the oldest buildings in the north-east, was reserved for their own private use in memory of a son who had drowned.

The burgh was granted royal status by Mary Queen of Scots in 1563, thereby removing it from the authority of two rival factions. Her charter gave the townspeople the right to hold a weekly market and two fairs a year, and to administer their own court and engage in continental trade.

The nearby Water of Rattray was still navigable by ships at this time and the town rapidly developed as a consequence of its trading activities. The small, sheltered harbour was prone to silting up, however, and by 1650 trade was beginning to dwindle. The end came in 1720 when a massive storm blew up, permanently cutting the harbour off from the sea.

Much of Rattray was engulfed in sand. At the same time, the waterway began to silt up and with the harbour no longer viable, little attempt was made to dig out the settlement (which was then abandoned) or to restore the castle.

Ravenser Odd

East Riding of Yorkshire

IF RATTRAY FELL PREY TO SHIFTING SANDS, IT WAS water that did for the strangely named Ravenser Odd. A medieval port that once stood on the sandbanks at the mouth of the Humber river, it is now lost beneath the North Sea.

Knowing what we know now, its position sounds precarious, occupying as it does the far end of a long promontory that the Vikings knew as *Hrafn's Eyr* or the Raven's Tongue. But in the 1200s this was a fine location and Ravenser Odd was clearly a thriving and important town as a consequence.

'With many fisheries and the most abundantly provided with ships and burgesses of all the boroughs of that coast', its merchants (according to a fourteenth-century monk at the local Meaux Abbey) were richer and more successful than those of the nearby king's town of Kingston upon Hull. Well placed not just for trade but also for fishing and for provisioning visiting vessels, the people of Ravenser Odd became renowned for something called forestalling. This was the art of persuading captains of passing ships to unload in their own town rather than continuing on to Grimsby or Hull.

It was perhaps to this somewhat sharp practice that the same monk was alluding when he described the town's 'wicked deeds and especially wrong-doings on the sea'. 'By its evil actions and predations,' he insisted, 'it provoked the vengeance of God upon itself beyond measure.'

The vengeance, if indeed that's what it was, came in the form of repeated incursions by the North Sea. What had been the source of Ravenser Odd's great wealth now turned to become its great enemy. More than once several of the one hundred or so houses were flooded, along with its church, warehouses, quays and other harbour buildings. Repairing these took time and cost money, and trade began to suffer as ships sailed on to safer, more resilient ports.

The final blow came in January 1362 with the *Grote Mandrenke* or Great Drowning (see England's Atlantis, page 51). When a ferocious south-westerly storm combined with unusually high tides, the sandbanks shifted, carrying what remained of the town out to sea. So little was left behind that Ravenser Odd might almost never have been there in the first place.

A Really Huge Naked Lady

Northumberland

IT WOULD BE DIFFICULT TO LOSE THE COUNTRY'S largest nude figure – head to toe she's 400 metres long and is thought to weigh 1.5 million tonnes – but beneath her curvaceous contours lies the lost landscape of a former coalmine.

Also known as the Big Bird or, more rudely, Slag Alice, Britain's biggest sculpture was designed to be walked on. More than

four miles of footpaths snake their way around the body and limbs of *Northumberlandia*, allowing visitors to explore the £3 million creation and enjoy clambering up the raised portions of her forehead, breasts, hip, knee and ankles.

To give some indication of scale, this latest angel of the north has a four-metre-long nose. She was designed by American landscape architect and designer Charles Jencks in a collaborative venture with a mining company and the science writer the 5th Viscount Ridley. As a significant local landowner, Ridley was looking for an alternative to the usual means of disposing of a redundant mine, which too often involves returning the site to nature (with varying degrees of success) or recasting it as an ugly industrial estate.

The Big Bird was also meant as a gift to the local community, 2,500 of whom had objected to the mine when it was first mooted but now find themselves with a highly idiosyncratic public park from the top of which one is rewarded with stupendous views of the sea and the Cheviot Hills.

River Medlock

Manchester

LONDON FAMOUSLY HAS MANY LOST RIVERS, among them the Effra, Fleet and Devil's Neckinger. In Manchester, the equivalent missing waterway is the Medlock, which rises in the hills near Oldham but disappears somewhere beneath the bustling metropolis.

Eventually it joins the River Irwell and reaches the sea by way of the Mersey. But just as London's secret rivers have been engineered almost out of existence – several are now sewers, at least one of which can be seen passing over the platforms at Sloane Square station in a huge pipe – the route of the Medlock is now far from the one that nature had intended.

At a few points in the city it can be sighted momentarily, for example below a bridge near Piccadilly Station and then again before it disappears beneath the old Gaythorn gasworks. But it has not been navigable since the early nineteenth century and, at one point, the water was found to be so polluted that it was considered too filthy to be allowed to join the city's famous Bridgewater Canal. Little wonder, perhaps, in an area the Marxist Friedrich Engels described as 'the most horrible' during his examination of working-class life in the city in the 1840s. Little wonder, too, that the decision was taken for it to join the 9,000 miles of rivers that were rerouted or diverted underground by the builders of our great Victorian cities.

Nicknamed the 'red river' for the high levels of pollution from a nearby abattoir, periodic floods only redoubled the horror such as when, for example, it washed away corpses from an adjacent Roman Catholic cemetery in 1872. Driving it underground into newly built brick channels must have seemed like the only choice open to the city fathers, but as a result of this many Mancunians have never heard of the Medlock, let alone seen it for themselves.

Roxburgh

Roxburghshire

REPEATEDLY CAPTURED, RECAPTURED AND ransacked by both sides in Scotland's wars of independence, this former royal burgh and sometimes capital was eventually destroyed in the mid-1400s but never rebuilt.

Supposedly well located in the midst of the rich farmland of the Borders, Roxburgh's position on what ought to have been a readily defensible spot between the Tweed and Teviot rivers meant it was bound to attract the attention of invaders.

The town was relatively rich, thanks to the trade in goods travelling inland along the first of these rivers from the port at Berwick-upon-Tweed, and for much of the reign of David I (1124–53) it effectively served as the Scottish capital as the king chose to make his home there.

Roxburgh's principal defensive point was its castle, a royal stronghold that first surrendered to the English in 1174 and later changed hands several times, including once when it was captured by Scotsmen supposedly disguised as cows. In 1460, it was destroyed by another group of Scots, apparently fearful that if they lost it to the English again the latter would be able to use it to overrun the whole region.

The same Scottish troops successfully laid siege to the town, although with the loss of King James II who was killed when one of his own cannons exploded. Ruling in his place for the next three years, his widow, Mary of Guelders, who may have actually encouraged the destruction of the castle, and the town never recovered from the slight. Once the English had taken Berwick for the final time, trade on the river ground to a halt and, losing its revenues and much of its purpose, the town went into decline. Soon afterwards it ceased to exist, its name passing to a village a couple of miles away, but without its predecessor's prestige.

The Royal Military Canal

Kent

A SLENDER RIBBON OF WATER BARELY TEN METRES **wide is all that remains of elaborate plans to flood a great swathe of southern England to thwart an ambitious Corsican adventurer.**

At first telling it seems extraordinary that anyone would suppose a mere canal could stop an army that had already crossed the Channel (not to mention the Danube and Rhine), but in a sense that was precisely what was being asked of the Royal Military Canal.

Napoleon Bonaparte was convinced that the conquest of England was the key to his plans to dominate Europe, insisting all he needed was 'a favourable wind to plant the Imperial Eagle on the Tower of London'. Facing an invasion by as many as 130,000 troops, the authorities in England knew they had to move fast.

Attention focused on Romney Marsh, an extensive, low-lying region of Kent that was thought the most likely place for any invasion to begin. Despite this, the area had been left

largely undefended, on the grounds that it was boggy and liable to flood and therefore not easy for an army to cross. Now, staring down the barrels of so many guns, as it were, this assumption was questioned and found wanting.

Fortifying the area and defending such a long stretch of coastline was clearly no longer an option. Instead it was decided to excavate a canal around the back of the marsh, running nearly twenty miles from Seabrook near Folkestone to the River Rother at Rye.

Nineteen metres wide and three deep, the spoil could be heaped up behind the canal, providing an arrangement not dissimilar to Hadrian's Wall, forcing the would-be invader to attack uphill and providing defenders with a raised parapet from which to fire.

Time and cost constraints eventually dictated a canal only half this width, but the theory seemed sound. After seeing plans, the prime minister expressed his confidence in the scheme (which thereafter became known as Mr Pitt's Ditch) and work began in October 1804.

Progress on the canal was slow, however, and things remained fraught even when the army took over from civilian contractors. Fortunately, Bonaparte was forced to rein in his plans following his defeat at Trafalgar in 1805 and so the canal was never needed. Unfortunately, it had cost the Exchequer well over £230,000 – an almost incalculable sum and one that proved impossible to recover, even once the canal was thrown open to the public and tolls charged.

Royal Touch

London

FOR CENTURIES IT WAS BELIEVED THAT MERELY touching a sovereign would cure skin diseases such as scrofula, and until 1714 and the accession of the Elector of Hanover, Britain regularly engaged with a most peculiar form of folk medicine.

George's decision not to follow the example of the late Queen Anne had nothing to do with his continental origins, as what was known as touching for the king's evil continued in Europe until well into the 1800s. French kings seem to have been particular enthusiasts, and Henry IV of France (1553–1610) once admitted more than 1,500 subjects into his presence at a single sitting.

Perhaps the greatest surprise is not the naive belief that it might do any good for sufferers of scrofula, a tubercular

condition, but rather that any king or queen would agree to touch a commoner. In fact, while by no means the norm, such events were not without precedent and the idea of sovereigns being untouchable is a relatively recent one.

Today we think of the ceremony known as Maundy Thursday as involving no more than the presentation of specially minted coins to pensioners as a personal gift from the queen. But historically the affair was far more intimate and until the reign of Mary I (1553–8), it had been traditional for the sovereign to come down from the throne to wash the feet of the assembled commoners in a clear imitation of Christ administering to his disciples at the Last Supper. Only after this had been done would the coins have been presented.

The number of commoners was chosen to reflect the monarch's age, meaning more than forty of them at Bloody Mary's last. Additionally, modest amounts of money were distributed, along with bread and fish (another biblical echo) and a small portion of the royal robe. Her successor Elizabeth, apparently tiring of the squabbles over the latter, decided to dispense with the practice and simply arranged for those present to receive a monetary gift.

The giving of Maundy money has survived to this day, and the coins themselves are highly sought after. But the Royal Touch died with Queen Anne in 1714. Among those she touched was the future Dr Johnson, but finding the whole thing 'too Catholic', her successor George I refused to play along.

The Saunders-Roe Princess

Isle of Wight

ANOTHER OF BRITISH AVIATION'S GREAT WHITE elephants, Europe's largest ever flying boat was cancelled before two of the three built had even taken off.

The concept of the flying boat made a lot of sense in the 1930s when conventional runways were thin on the ground. With characteristic perversity Benito Mussolini built a water runway far inland near Milan (renamed Idroscalo, it's now a watersports centre) but, otherwise, the appeal of flying boats depended on nearly three-quarters of the planet being covered by water.

This meant they could land almost anywhere. Taking off from Lake Victoria, the luxurious C-Class Empire 'boats' of Imperial Airways had a runway the length of Ireland, and without any of the expense of planning, earth-moving and civil engineering that was needed to translate field and forest into a viable commercial aerodrome.

The arguments for the boats were compelling in wartime, too. A self-contained fighting unit that could patrol for literally days at a time, the fortitude of the Short Sunderland earned the respect of Luftwaffe pilots who nicknamed it *fliegendes Stachelschwein* (flying porcupine) for its formidable armoury of more than a dozen large-calibre machine guns.

But after six years of war, the situation had swung through 180 degrees. Now Europe had thousands of military runways, and enormous technological advances had improved the reliability, range and speed of conventional land-based aircraft. Suddenly the flying boats that had once mastered the globe looked like antiquated relics of a world everybody wished to leave behind.

In America, Spruce Goose, which Howard Hughes had designed to carry more than 700 passengers, was mothballed

after a single maiden flight of barely a mile. Most of the rest were unceremoniously scrapped, including Britain's futuristic contender, the mighty ten-engined Princess. The last great flourish of a proud history of marine aviation, only its instruments were kept to be reused by the cross-Channel SR.N4 hovercraft – a far more humdrum machine, with neither the Saro's grace nor its pace.

The Scapa Flow Scuttling

Orkney

THE SUDDEN LOSS OF THE GERMAN HIGH Seas Fleet was one of the most surprising events of the Great War, not least because it was entirely self-inflicted.

The largest flotilla of fighting ships ever to set sail from British shores did so ten days after the war had ended. Operation ZZ saw nearly 200 battleships, cruisers and destroyers heading out into the North Sea to rendezvous with the might of the Imperial German Navy.

Their task was to take nine battleships into custody, together with five battlecruisers, seven cruisers and fifty destroyers. The world's second largest fleet (after the Royal Navy) was being handed over to its sworn enemy as a condition of the German surrender.

For the Admiralty, this overwhelming show of strength was a chance to underline how, in a war that began with a naval arms race, the strategic defeat of German seapower had perhaps made an even greater contribution to victory than any single battle fought on land. For the Germans it was an utter disaster, a day of pain and shame on which their ships were consigned to Scapa Flow, Orkney's great natural harbour.

Negotiations were underway as to the vessels' eventual fate, but as these dragged on into the following year, those left on board began to formulate a plan of their own. The nature of this became clear on 21 June when Admiral von Reuter gave the order to scuttle. Stopcocks were opened, waterpipes ruptured, and by late afternoon fifty-two vessels lay on the bottom of the sea. Tragically, in the chaos, nine German sailors were shot and killed, but nearly 1,800 were rescued and sent to prison camps on the mainland.

For the Royal Navy, struggling to maintain its own fleet, it was a problem solved. For Germany it was an honourable and dignified response to an intolerable situation, and today divers are able to swim over those wrecks that were not salvaged and scrapped. The only real losers were the French, who had hoped to acquire a fine new navy at no cost to themselves.

The 7th Earl of Lucan

East Sussex

BRITAIN'S MOST FAMOUS FUGITIVE HAS BEEN
lost for more than forty years but, despite
numerous sightings at exotic locations around
the world, he probably made it no further than
the south coast.

The last confirmed sighting of his lordship was in November 1974, by which time the committed but failing gambler was estranged from his wife and living alone in London. When his children's nanny was murdered, he came under immediate suspicion, the assumption being that he had let himself into the family's Belgravia home and mistaken Sandra Rivett for his wife.

From the newspapers' perspective, the decidedly Cluedo-esque killing had it all, from a bloodied length of lead piping to an authentically aristocratic prime suspect. That the latter managed to disappear into thin air was the icing on the cake, particularly when it was rumoured that a rich and powerful elite were looking after their own and had spirited their chum out of the country.

The fact he left London without a passport did nothing to derail this idea, nor the discovery of a borrowed Ford Corsair that he had abandoned at Newhaven. Reports of Lucan lookalikes started to come in thick and fast, initially from France and Holland, then Ireland, South Africa, Australia and even India.

The likelihood, however, is that the former Guards officer was already dead. Were he not, he'd be in his eighties now, but there was nothing about his personality to suggest he would fare well on his own, would want to, or even had the emotional resources to carve out a new life for himself once this one went pear-shaped. In the absence of a body, Richard John Bingham was legally declared dead only in 1992, but the chances are that having dumped the car he realized his goose was cooked and drowned somewhere in the English Channel.

The Silver City Air Ferry

Kent

**IN THE 1950s, WHEN ADVENTURER HAMISH MOFFAT
set out to drive 12,000 miles from London to
Cape Town in an ancient Lagonda, he crossed to
France using a lost route whose memory those
who remember still mourn.**

With just a compass and the stars to navigate the Sahara,
blocks of wood in place of suspension and the unwanted
attentions of a ravenous lion when the old car shed a wheel,
Moffat's escapade reads like a fight for survival, although to
begin with, at least, he travelled in style.

Until being edged out by ghastly roll-on-roll-off ferries,
retired air commodore 'Taffy' Powell offered Moffat and
others who could afford it the possibility of flying their cars
to France. The speed and expense of Silver City's service
imbued it with an air of glamour, even when its grass airstrip
at Lympne in Kent became waterlogged.

To overcome this, the company relocated to Lydd
Ferryfield, the first civilian airport to be built in Britain
after the Second World War. Its fleet comprised a series of
ungainly but capacious cargo planes with bulbous noses that
swung open to admit cars bound for Le Touquet.

Only two or three could be accommodated per flight,
hence the relatively high cost, but by 1960 Silver City was
transporting an impressive 90,000 vehicles a year. It was
struggling financially, however, and two years later was taken
over. Investment in AT Carvairs, the same aircraft used by

the eponymous villain to transport his Rolls-Royce in the film *Goldfinger*, meant five cars could be carried. But these faced increased competition from seaborne ferries and soon hovercraft as well. With one cheaper and the other faster, cars gradually gave way to cargo and Britain's last air ferry took off on New Year's Day 1977.

St Kilda

Outer Hebrides

THE TINY ATLANTIC ARCHIPELAGO IS NOT SO much lost as exceptionally difficult to reach, since the evacuation of the last islanders more than eighty years ago.

A handful of weapons technicians work here in shifts, together with the occasional scientist or conservationist when the weather allows. But no one actually lives on Hirta any longer, the largest of the islands and the only one to have been settled in living memory.

Forty miles west of the Outer Hebrides, life on the shattered remains of a long-extinct volcano was never anything better than tough. Almost nothing grows there, most of the islanders' protein came from killing seagulls, and there was insufficient peat to heat the most primitive homes in the country. In more than 2,000 years of human habitation, the population rarely exceeded 150 and it dipped to just four adults and a dozen or so children when cholera and smallpox epidemics struck the islands in the 1720s.

For the islanders, the golden period was probably during the Great War when the Royal Navy sent over a detachment for the duration. This meant regular deliveries of food, coal and mail for the first and last time in the community's history, but when the sailors eventually withdrew it only heightened the community's sense of isolation.

Following a particularly hard winter in which several more died, they petitioned the government to help them leave. With only thirty-six of them left, it was difficult to refuse, and it can't have been much of a logistical challenge moving so few people with such meagre possessions. But looking at the abandoned line of roofless stone dwellings, one gets a sense that something significant has been lost, even if one has no real desire to stay behind long enough to find out what it is.

St Peter's Seminary

Dunbartonshire

BARELY FORTY TWENTIETH-CENTURY SCOTTISH buildings are rated as being of the highest architectural importance, so it comes as a shock to find that one of them was abandoned just a few years after its completion and is already a ruin.

The Roman Catholic seminary at Cardross was completed in 1966, its rough-cast concrete finish perhaps seen as the nearest modern equivalent of traditional Scottish harling, in which a building is weatherproofed with a coating of lime render mixed with small stone chips or pebbles. As an exemplar of brutalist building design, it has since been described as Scotland's greatest single post-war building, and even has an RIBA Gold Medal to prove it.

Unfortunately, the new building let in water and was expensive to maintain. It was also far too large for the Church at a time when the number of men seeking to train for the priesthood was in rapid decline. Accordingly, in 1980, the few remaining students were transferred elsewhere, and after a short period as a drug rehabilitation centre, the building closed its doors, beginning its disappearance back into the surrounding 140 acres of ancient woodland.

Stocks and Pillories

County Down

NEWSPAPERS OFTEN TALK OF PEOPLE BEING PILLORIED
**when they are named and shamed, but the
practice of publicly disgracing offenders in this
way was formally abandoned in 1837.**

As a popular figure, the writer Daniel Defoe was pelted with fresh flowers when he spent three hours in the pillory for seditious libel in 1703, but the ammunition of choice was typically rotten and rather more substantial. In earlier times a person sentenced to be punished this way might also have his ears cropped (cut) or nailed to the wooden boards used to restrain his neck and wrists.

Notwithstanding this sort of refinement, the punishment is sometimes regarded as mild or slightly comical, especially in

the case of stocks, which allowed the offender to sit down. It is also true that both means were generally used to punish those convicted of only relatively minor crimes, and that towards the end their use was restricted still further to cases of perjury.

The last Englishman to be punished this way was given a choice of being transported to Australia for seven years or spending an hour in the pillory. Peter Bossy chose the latter, unsurprisingly perhaps, but few of those restrained in this manner found much to laugh about.

The punishment could go on for several days and, far from being simply humiliated, criminals could be seriously injured by a mob determined to take advantage of the former's inability to defend themselves. It wasn't uncommon for individuals to be pelted with dead cats or have their faces smeared with excrement; others were maimed for life or even killed by flying bricks and stones.

Surviving sets of pillories are unusual, and in Suffolk at Thorpe Morieux is an even rarer example, which doubles up as the village sign. But stocks have fared rather better and at least two dozen examples can still be seen in churchyards and on village greens up and down the country. Most are of wood but at Dromore in Northern Ireland, a particularly good set made of wrought iron is positioned outside the old market house.

Stow Maries Aerodrome

Essex

THOUGH PRIMITIVE AND UNRELIABLE, BRITISH aircraft played a key role in the Great War, yet every airfield from the period has been lost, with the exception of this one precious survivor.

Until they were amalgamated after the war to form the RAF, the army's Royal Flying Corps and the Royal Naval Air Service operated independently of each other, and there was considerable rivalry between the two. Curiously, the navy could boast that it had the first mechanized land force – a fleet of Rolls-Royce Silver Ghost armoured cars – but the RFC had more aircraft and many more airfields.

At their peak there were dozens of airfields in Britain,

and of course temporary ones in France, as well. Today all have disappeared but one, some lost beneath housing and industrial estates, others returned to the open farmland they were before the war, and at least one of which developed into a thriving commercial airport.

Many others were retained by the new Royal Air Force, but subsequent expansion to cope with better, faster and more numerous machines – particularly during the Second World War – means that every trace of the old RFC was obliterated. Only Stow Maries has survived, and much more by chance than design.

Located on the Dengie peninsular formed by the rivers Blackwater and Crouch, the airfield opened in 1916 and was used by 37 Squadron defending London from Zeppelin attacks. Considered surplus to requirements at war's end, it was thought unsuitable for development in the Second World War and slipped off the radar. Most of the site was returned to agriculture, but happily no attempt was made to demolish any of the wartime buildings, which soon became overgrown.

It took until 2009 for these to be identified and, now owned by a couple of aviation enthusiasts, two dozen of them have been Grade II-listed to ensure their survival. With a recent National Heritage Memorial Fund grant to help with their restoration, Stow Maries lives on as a unique memorial to the first real war in the air.

Temperance Bars

Lancashire

THEME PUBS ARE POPULAR, BUT IT SEEMS UNLIKELY
that many people would think of opening one
now that didn't serve alcohol. In the nineteenth
century, such pubs were far from rare, and
particularly in Yorkshire and Lancashire they
enjoyed quite a long run of success.

At the time of writing, the 120-year-old Mr Fitzpatrick's in Rawtenstall is the only survivor of hundreds that sprang up as part of a wider temperance movement in Victorian England. Asked to sign a pledge agreeing to refrain from the demon drink, customers were offered Vimto, ginger beer and sarsaparilla as alternatives, as well as tastier-sounding treats such as blackbeer and raisin, lemon and ginger, and something called blood tonic.

Although there was a definite religious tinge to it all (the Methodists were keen supporters), much of the impetus came from industry. For example, the British Association for the Promotion of Temperance was founded in 1835, a time when increasing industrialization needed workers who would not only get up every morning, but be sober enough to operate complex and potentially dangerous machinery.

Before long, most towns in the north had at least one temperance bar, but not everyone was happy to sign the pledge, however, and with intoxication still considered a social taboo, the restriction of pub opening hours was to form part of the 1914 Defence of the Realm Act. In fact, by then the temperance movement was well on the wane, and after the Second World War the remaining interest rapidly fell away. Once cheap, sugary colas began to be imported in bulk from the US, drinks like dandelion and burdock began to sound quaint. Before long, only Mr Fitzpatrick's was left, offering a little of the flavour of what has been lost.

Tide Mills

East Sussex

A HUNDRED-YEAR-OLD EXPERIMENTAL SEAPLANE BASE HAS **almost entirely disappeared, together with a village that grew up around an eighteenth-century mill.**

As the name suggests, the mill was powered by the ebb and flow of the tide, an unusual arrangement of which only three working examples survive in Britain. This particular one was built on land owned by the 1st Duke of Newcastle in 1761, towards the end of his time as prime minister, and remained in use for the next 120 years.

Large and powerful, with three wheels and sixteen sets of stones for grinding flour, it was later equipped with a system of winches driven by a windmill. Suggesting something of an industrial complex, it eventually acquired many subsidiary buildings housing a blacksmith, a carpentry shop and a large granary.

All this took considerable manpower to operate, and clustered around the working buildings the aforementioned village quickly developed to provide living accommodation.

Soon the workforce was producing thousands of sacks of flour every week, and by 1879 there was even a station here on the Newhaven to Seaford line called Tide Mills Halt.

In 1883, however, the wheels stopped turning and the old mill closed. The railway had made it more economical for local farmers to send their grain elsewhere, and work on the harbour at Newhaven prevented larger vessels tying up at the mill to load and unload. For a few years the buildings were used for storage, but when the railway line was torn up in 1901, demolition seemed the only option.

The village limped on a while longer, but in the late 1930s the houses were condemned as unfit for living. They probably were – water came from standpipes and sewage went into the sea – and clearing what Fleet Street dubbed 'the hamlet of horror' suited the authorities very well. In 1940, the remaining buildings were torn down, and troops moved in as part of Britain's wartime coastal defence. The civilians never returned, and with nothing left it seems unlikely anyone will now.

Trolleybuses

West Riding of Yorkshire

ESSENTIALLY A TRAM THAT COULD GO OFF-PISTE,
the trolleybus drew its power from the same
overhead cables as its predecessor and plied the
streets of fifty British towns and cities.

The world's first trolleybus was built in Berlin in the 1880s,

although it was nearly thirty years before a British municipal authority introduced something similar. Here, Bradford took the lead in 1911 and was also the last place in the country to operate a trolleybus service before bringing down the shutters in 1972.

Better able to cope with a hilly terrain than a tram, trolleybuses, being trackless, also required less infrastructure and in the event of a breakdown could be pushed to one side rather than blocking the route. Rubber tyres meant they were also much quieter and (although this was not a major consideration in the early days) running on electricity kept air pollution out of city centres as the power was generated elsewhere.

Of course there were disadvantages. Overhead wires and supports ruined the appearance of many historic towns (particularly where two or more streets crossed) and it was impossible for the trolleybus to drive around an obstruction if the next street had no wires. Trolleybuses were also unable to overtake each other, and occasionally – as happened with trams – one could become disconnected from the overhead wire and roll to a halt.

Conventional diesel buses avoided all this and, although their engines were noisy and smelly, they offered operators much greater flexibility. Ignoring the health risks, they must have seemed superior in almost every regard, and gradually trolleybus services began to be withdrawn in Britain. Forty other countries still use them, but this country's last made its final scheduled journey on 26 March 1972. Somehow escaping the scrapheap, No.758 is currently being restored to working condition.

TSR-2

Shropshire

BRITAIN'S MOST AMBITIOUS AIRCRAFT DESIGN WAS lost to political meddling, inter-service squabbles and the massive cost overruns that always seem to dog major military projects.

Equipped to launch nuclear strikes and for undertaking advanced reconnaissance missions, the TSR-2 was very much the British aviation industry's last hurrah, after which it never again attempted to build a front-line aircraft of its own.

At the height of the Cold War, new Soviet surface-to-air missiles meant the RAF could no longer rely on flying high to avoid enemy contact. This called for an entirely new generation of aircraft and, in 1960, the British Aircraft Corporation was formed by merging independent players such as English Electric and Vickers-Armstrong.

BAC's TSR-2 was going to be crucial to its success: a machine able to fly low at mach speeds, penetrate enemy defences and attack high-value targets with both nuclear and conventional weapons. At the same time, world-beating technology would enable it to gather vital photo-imagery and signals intelligence.

The first prototype, *XR219*, took to the air in late 1964, only for the project to be killed off just six months later. The decision was made on April Fool's Day, the new Labour government effectively dealing a death blow to British aviation when it chose to buy aircraft from its American rivals instead.

How good the TSR-2 was is impossible to say. Of the twenty-three airframes partly or completely finished, only the prototype flew, and the cancellation is still so controversial that no one has a truly objective, untainted opinion even now. Probably Sir Sydney Camm came closest, the designer of the Hurricane and the Harrier jump-jet wryly noting that 'modern aircraft have four dimensions: span, length, height and politics. TSR-2 simply got the first three right.'

RAF Museum Cosford has one of two survivors on display. The other is at the Imperial War Museum, Duxford.

Tuberculosis Hospital

Warwickshire

**An old, abandoned children's hospital in
Coleshill carries an eerie reminder of a time
when a killer stalked the land.**

Its wards still littered with patients' personal effects as well as bloodstained medical equipment, trolleys and broken beds, St Gerard's Hospital in north Warwickshire looks for all the world as if everyone stepped out one day without realizing that they would never be returning.

Over many decades until its closure in 1988, St Gerard's treated thousands of sick children, many of them victims of consumption or TB, a debilitating and often fatal illness which, at its peak, affected more than 50,000 people a year in Britain alone.

Spread by coughs and sneezes, its symptoms have been found in the remains of 5,000-year-old Egyptian mummies, although the illness was only identified in 1882. Left untreated, as many as half of those infected die, and until the use of antibiotics became widespread in the mid-twentieth century, the usual treatment was to pack those afflicted off to sanitoriums for long periods of rest and fresh air and to hope for the best.

Patients often spent months and sometimes years in such places. Typically they were lined up outside for much of the time, even on days when snow was falling in the belief that the best remedy was cold, clean, country air. (Bizarrely some patients also had heavy sandbags placed on their chests, giving their damaged lungs something to push against.)

The arrival of penicillin (in the form of streptomycin) in the 1940s changed this approach, although hospitals like St Gerard's remained in business for several decades more. By the 1980s, TB cases in Britain had fallen by as much as 90 per cent and while most of the old hospitals were demolished or redeveloped, a few like St Gerard's were left to slowly decay.

Tyneham

Dorset

WITH EVIDENCE THAT IT WAS SETTLED AS long ago as the Iron Age, south Dorset's most famous lost village was forcibly cleared of inhabitants and closed in 1943.

The order came from the War Office, which was keen to secure the surrounding country as a training ground and military firing range. More than 200 villagers were required to relocate, and did so in the belief that they would be allowed back to their homes once the war had reached its end. A handwritten message was even left on the church door to this effect, reminding soldiers 'to treat the church and houses with care. We have given up our homes where many of us lived for generations to help win the war to keep men free. We shall return one day and thank you for treating the village kindly.'

It was certainly on this understanding that around 8,000

acres were commandeered for the army but then, following the defeat of Germany, the MoD decided to retain what had turned out to be a superbly useful military facility. Moves were made to compulsorily purchase the whole lot – including the village and church – and wartime banning orders were swiftly renewed. By 1950, members of the public, including villagers, were still forbidden to enter the area.

The plight of the locals became more widely known over the next few years, and with a campaign calling for some limited access to the area, it was finally decided in 1975 to amend the original regulations. There was still no question of regaining the village, but from then on some public footpaths were reopened each summer or when the range was not in use, albeit with warning signs about unexploded ordnance.

To even the most blinkered visitor, however, it is apparent that not everything has been treated with the care the villagers were hoping for. The wildlife in the area is certainly thriving, suggesting regular shelling causes less distress to flora and fauna than do the normal everyday activities of man. But the same cannot be said of the village, in which several buildings have been badly damaged by shellfire and arguably the best of them, the Elizabethan manor, actually torn down.

St Mary's Church, at least, was undamaged (it is now a museum), along with the tiny village school and an exceptionally rare 1920s 'K1' telephone box. That said, the latter is a replacement, the original having been destroyed accidentally by one of the many film-makers drawn to this unique, if mournful, setting. Unfortunately, it was one of only half a dozen survivors of the more than 6,300 originals, which have been lost.

Victoria

County of Perth

**AN ASTONISHING COLLECTION OF NEARLY
900,000 old nails is all that remains of a lost
Roman fortress, which was constructed in the
first century AD as part of a campaign against the
barbarian hordes of Caledonia.**

Also known as Pinnata Castra, the fort was built at speed but in use for no more than five years. Covering an area of more than fifty acres overlooking the north bank of the Tay River, it served as the headquarters of governor Gnaeus Julius Agricola and once housed more than 5,000 men of the Legion XX Valeria Victrix.

In AD 86, however, the legion was ordered south and a decision was taken to destroy the fort. To prevent them being used by Rome's enemies, more than sixty barracks were burned to the ground, together with subsidiary buildings housing workshops and an army hospital. Unwanted military equipment and personal effects were similarly smashed to pieces, and every effort made to ensure that nothing was left behind that might prove useful.

A total of 875,400 iron and steel nails used to construct the extensive wooden walls posed a major problem, however. They represented a technology the Picts didn't yet have, a technology that had enabled the Romans to engineer the world's greatest empire with all its bridges, ships, aquaducts and swords. But they also weighed a tonne – more than seven tonnes, in fact – making them impossibly heavy to move.

Instead it was decided to dig a deep pit and throw the

whole lot in, and it was the discovery of this pit that caused the most excitement when the site was first excavated by a team of archaeologists in the 1950s. The press and public might have preferred more obvious treasure, a hoard of precious gold coins, perhaps, or jewels. But to archaeologists, this was treasure of another kind, something that provided clues as to the scale of the fort which once stood here and of Agricola's operations.

At Inchtuthil today there is almost nothing to see of Victoria, but it is thrilling nevertheless to stand on what was once the far edge of the Roman Empire. Beneath the rough grass lies the only legionary fortress in the whole of the empire where the outline plan has not been disturbed by later building. It may be lost, but we know it's there.

Village Lock-up

Somerset

Probably rather more effective than an asbo, the village lock-up dates back to a time when justice was administered locally and usually without delay.

A few have survived, and the one at Castle Cary in Somerset is popularly supposed to have provided the inspiration for the traditional 'custodian helmet' worn by the police. But the overwhelming majority have been pulled down, with only a few 'repurposed', such as the one at Wirksworth in Derbyshire, which is a bed and breakfast, and another twenty miles away in Curbar, which became a cottage.

It wasn't unusual for lock-ups to be built in whichever was the fashionable architectural style of the time, especially where the expense was borne by a local landowner rather than the parish council. But behind any aesthetic flourishes, most were fairly basic buildings, typically comprising a single, small room with a barred window (if any window at all) and absolutely nothing in the way of creature comforts.

Offenders were usually guilty of something minor, often drunks who were released the following morning, but those accused of a more serious offence could also be kept locked up in them until they could be brought before a magistrate. References to their use goes back a long way – the City of London had a lock-up on Cornhill in the thirteenth century –

but peak usage came in the eighteenth and nineteenth centuries and it is from this period that most of the survivors date.

Reviving the use of local lock-ups is considered from time to time, if only by the same people who wish to see a return to National Service or public hanging. However, it's unlikely that such a simple remedy for bad behaviour could work in this age of protected human rights and, as such, lock-ups are surely consigned to be a relic of the past.

'Waddling to the Waters'

Somerset

AT A TIME WHEN PEOPLE PAY MORE FOR BOTTLED water than for petrol, milk or beer, it is odd that the fashion for taking the waters has not seen another revival in recent years.

The waddling phrase came from the writer Horace Walpole, a cruel depiction of the fashionable but presumably fat upper-class clientele of Britain's many spa towns, whom he said spent so much time in them they would be mistaken for ducks.

The habit started with the Romans, unsurprisingly, who, seeking a Rome from Rome, as it were, created England's first spa town. What they called Aquae Sulis was quickly established as a place of leisure and luxury, and in 1676 a successful quack-doctor called Thomas Guidott published his *Discourse of Bathe, and the Hot Waters There. Also, Some Enquiries into the Nature of the Water*. Later came the social entrepreneur Richard 'Beau' Nash and two classically minded architects called Wood who, between them, transformed the city into the best of Georgian England's resorts.

Buoyed up by waters pouring forth at a rate of more than a million litres a day (still through Roman plumbing) and a wavering 46°C, Bath became rich. Where it led, others followed, and from Ashbourne to Woodhall Spa there were soon more than fifty towns and cities in which the aristocrats and their followers could take the waters. Fresh or saline, hot or cold, and at least at Harrogate 'clear as crystal but foetid and nauseous to the smell', the mineral springs were said to cure a multiplicity of conditions in anyone who drank or immersed themselves in the stuff.

Curiously, it was the spas' growing popularity that killed them off in the end: new railway lines made it possible for too many of the wrong social classes to engage in some waddling of their own. Spas that had once been the height of fashion became places where (as one snobbish observer noted) the properly sick 'were sent by lower-class doctors to cough away their misery in backstreet lodgings'. Before long the bubble burst, and the craze dried up.

Wade's Roads

Scottish Highlands

IN THE EARLY 1700S, AN EXTENSIVE NETWORK OF military roads opened up the Highlands for the first time, but in the last 300 years many miles have been allowed to melt back into the landscape.

Named after the Anglo–Irish field marshal George Wade (1673–1748), they formed part of a concerted effort to assert control over an area of the country that had been causing the Hanoverians trouble since the 1715 Jacobite Uprising. New roads were seen as a key component of this, providing the means to rapidly move red-coated troops around the Highlands to combat the threat of as many as 12,000 clansmen bearing arms.

Appointed Commander-in-Chief, North Britain in 1724, General Wade as he then was drew up plans for 300 miles of new road linking Inverness and Fort William, Inverness and Dunkeld, Crieff and Dalnacardoch, and Dalwhinnie and Fort Augustus at the end of Loch Ness. Construction was to rigorously high standards, the cost of £90 a mile allowing for forty bridges (and the skilled carpenters and masons needed to build them) as well as firm foundations of large stones, layers of smaller stones above, and a top surface of well-drained gravel.[19]

Wages were unusually high, an indication of the

19. The Tay Bridge at Aberfeldy was the most expensive single structure. It cost £4,000 to build in 1734 and is still used today.

importance of the project, and most of the work was completed during the summer months to avoid the worst of the Highland weather. Midges remained a problem for the men, but what was by far the largest engineering scheme north of the border since Roman times was completed in 1740 when Wade quit Scotland.

Wade's success encouraged the government in London to pursue his ideas further still, and over the coming decades another 800 miles at least were built, mostly under a Major Caulfield. As Inspector of Roads for Scotland, he improved the quality of construction still further and, like Wade and the Romans before him, endeavoured wherever possible to build his roads arrow-straight.

Some Scots still argue the result was a bad thing: tax revenues went up, there were the Highland Clearances of a part of the population, and some of the more romantic qualities of clan life disappeared. But their usefulness and quality has ensured that stretches of these old roads have survived, and a glance at a map reveals several places where modern A roads follow Wade's routes almost exactly.

Much has been lost, however, which was perhaps inevitable once the Jacobite threat evaporated almost as quickly as it had materialized. As the need for the roads fell away, maintenance requirements weren't met and where there was no obvious civilian use, whole sections were abandoned. By the end of the eighteenth century an estimated 500 miles were no longer suitable for wagons or coaches, often because bridges had collapsed or been washed away by floods and not replaced.

Some of these can be travelled on foot, for example where short stretches serve as paths for hikers or as tracks crossing some of the great rural estates. A few other parts, for example the extension to the Crieff to Dalnacardoch road at the Corrieyairack Pass, are now protected ancient monuments. Here it is possible to appreciate the high quality of a substantially unaltered portion of Georgian civil engineering, but how strange to think that much of the Highlands are harder to reach now than they were in the eighteenth century.

Wentworth Woodhouse

West Riding of Yorkshire

THE LOSS OF ITS PARK AND A GREAT 15,000-ACRE estate means an uncertain future for Britain's largest private house.

For a long time one of the pictures most popular with visitors to the National Gallery was *Whistlejacket* by George Stubbs, a full-size portrait of a favourite horse belonging to an eighteenth-century prime minister, the 2nd Marquess of Rockingham. Nearly three metres square, its great size matches the house where it once hung, the more than 2.5 acre footprint of Wentworth Woodhouse encompassing five miles of corridors and a rumoured 365 rooms.

With a Palladian façade twice the width of Buckingham Palace, maintaining such a giant was always going to be challenging, and without the revenues of a large estate it might actually be impossible. Certainly since the Fitzwilliam family died out – the 6th earl had eight sons all called William, but the 10th died in 1979 without an heir – it has had its ups and downs.

In fact, its problems date back further, to 1946 when the government ordered the park and formal gardens to be torn up and for coal to be mined right up to the walls of the house. Even the miners were appalled at what they were being told to do, and with the Yorkshire branch president of the National Union of Mineworkers describing Wentworth Woodhouse as 'sacred ground', many locally still see it as a spiteful act of class warfare.

Notwithstanding the protests, more than 130,000 tonnes were extracted from the gardens alone, but it was low-grade stuff and the damage to Wentworth Woodhouse was irreversible. Life in the house became intolerable, so the family withdrew to another of its estates. At the same time extensive opencast mining dramatically reduced the attractiveness of Wentworth Woodhouse to visitors, and when it was offered to the National Trust they declined to take it on.

In this way it was unable to join Fountains Abbey, Castle Howard, Nostell Priory and Harewood on Yorkshire's booming post-war tourist trail, a failure described by architectural historians as a tragedy. Instead, after thirty years as a PE teacher training college, Wentworth Woodhouse was eventually sold to a millionaire businessman but then repossessed by a Swiss bank and put back on the market. In poor condition, it was bought and sold once more, probably for no more than £1.5 million, and at the time of writing it was back on the market again with just a few dozen acres. No price was given and *The Times* suggested any buyer would need to find an additional £40 million at least for vital remedial work.

West Tofts

Norfolk

THE NEED FOR A FAKE 'NAZI VILLAGE' MEANT THE death of several genuine English ones, and the loss of tens of thousands of acres when these were handed over to the army.

A few miles over the Norfolk–Suffolk boundary are road signs showing the way to Stanta or the Stanford Training Area, but since the Second World War a great swathe of East Anglia has been shrouded in secrecy. Creating what was then known as the Stanford Battle Area (if only to those who needed to know), almost fifty square miles of countryside north of Thetford were emptied of inhabitants, along with the villages of Buckenham Parva, Langford, Stanford, Sturston, Tottington, and West Tofts.

The vast acreage was required initially for tank exercises, and for training troops on the run-up to Operation Overlord (D-Day) in June 1944. Facilities at that time included the aforementioned Nazi village, carefully constructed to make the live-firing exercises as realistic as possible. A Cold War village followed a few years later; called Eastmere, it was built along East German lines, and a few years ago Stanta gained an Afghan one. Here, actors and former soldiers filled the roles of villagers in the mosque and at the market, the levels of verisimilitude apparently so good that troops were assailed by smells of rotting meat and raw sewage.

The real villagers have not been allowed to return for more than seventy years, however, although they are sometimes allowed visits for compassionate reasons, such as tending the grave of a family member in one of the four abandoned churches. The one at West Tofts has a nationally important A. W. N. Pugin interior and makes a thrilling, if poignant, stop on one of the rare guided tours offered to members of the public with a personal connection to the area.

Several architecturally less significant buildings have also survived; some have been modified for use by the army. But many have gone, including Buckenham Tofts Manor and its private cricket pitch, together with numerous medieval cottages, which are now little more than turfy humps on the ground. Much older remains, including Roman and Saxon sites, have fared rather better and, ecologically, the area is said to be thriving. But as a place where troops have trained to such good effect for service in Northern Ireland, the Falklands and Balkans, and latterly Iraq and Afghanistan, no one locally is expecting the military to hand back their lost villages anytime soon.

Wharram Percy

North Riding of Yorkshire

A ROOFLESS SHELL SURROUNDED BY mellowed, tilting gravestones, the ruin of St Martin's Church is a picturesque memorial to a lost North Yorkshire community.

Providing a stark contrast to the low green outline of Gains-thorpe (see page 57), the largely intact tower of the church is an unusually substantial relic by the normal standards of

British deserted medieval villages. Wharram Percy is also unusual in that it has been studied almost continually since its discovery shortly after the Second World War by a Leeds University professor.

An economist rather than an archaeologist, Maurice Beresford made the find in 1948 (his second) and returned each summer for the next forty years or more. With a team of archaeologists, historians and other specialists, he made a detailed study of the entire area, finding evidence of two substantial manor houses and 600 skeletons, as well as scores of peasant dwellings and farm buildings in a survey that has not been equalled anywhere in Europe.

His research suggests that the village existed in the ninth or tenth century, although there is evidence nearby of several Saxon, Romano-British and even Iron Age farmsteads. The richest villagers were probably of Viking descent when the village was mentioned in Domesday. Then it was known as 'Warron', the name only extended later when the village came under the control of the ambitious de Percy family.

The fortunes of both entities soon improved, the village growing in size and status and the family doing likewise so that today, more than 900 years after their arrival from France, the head is the 12th Duke of Northumberland. The village was also fortunate enough to escape the worst effects of the Black Death, although the number of residents had already begun to decline, perhaps as a consequence of land being given over to hunting (rather than crops) and sporadic but violent raids from north of the Scottish border.

A change of ownership briefly reversed the decline but by the early fifteenth century, only sixteen small houses were inhabited and the future looked far from rosy. With crop prices falling as fast as the value of wool rose, the agricultural landscape of northern England was shifting from being in the villagers' favour. We may owe the survival of the Grade I-listed church tower to their landlord Baron Hilton, but it was he who ordered the last few families to leave and in 1500 had their houses torn down. Their position usurped by over a thousand sheep and just two shepherds, Wharram Percy was dead.

Centuries later, a few of the fields still bear the names of what went before – including Towngate, Town Street and Water Lane – but there's precious little else to see beyond a millpond and the ruin of St Martin's.

The Williamson Tunnels

Liverpool

Mapped only in 1995 (and even then incompletely), Liverpudlians have a fascinating labyrinth running beneath their streets, but the reason for its existence is apparently lost for ever.

The existence of a network of early-nineteenth-century tunnels was known about before 1995, but until that date it was more or less impossible to enter because of the build-up of well over a century's worth of rubble and detritus. The tunnels owe their existence to a Yorkshireman called Joseph Williamson, who made a fortune trading in snuff and other tobacco products and spent some of the profits acquiring land in the Edge Hill area of the city.

Around 1805 he started building a number of reportedly eccentric houses on the land, none of which has survived intact, although the partial shell of one has been identified. These were intended for sale as well as for his own use, and the tunnelling is assumed to have begun as a means of forming gardens and terraces out of some old sandstone quarries he owned behind the houses.

The work needed to do this was considerable, and Williamson was soon employing a huge labour force. Many of the men are thought to have been returning soldiers from the Napoleonic wars, although there are no records to substantiate this. Building brick vaults over part of the quarry and moving spoil back and forth apparently at random, the men were kept busy for several decades until Williamson's death in 1840 at the age of seventy-one.

Williamson had been unhappily married and had no children, and work on the tunnels stopped as suddenly and as inexplicably as it had begun. By this time they were said to extend for several miles, typically running between three and five metres below the surface, but much like Williamson's houses, were built without any coherent plan or direction. No one knew for certain what they were meant for, and probably by now few cared. By 1867, a local newspaper was describing the labyrinth as a great nuisance, in large part because Victorian Scousers had begun using tunnels as a convenient dump for rubbish and an unstoppable flow of domestic effluent.

As the tunnels filled up with waste, they slowly slipped from memory and, in 1907, when a group of army reserves attempted to find a way through them they failed because many of the tunnels had become impassable. It took nearly ninety years before a second serious attempt was made to trace the tunnels, this time using electronic equipment to map the layout and the know-how of a Liverpool University geologist.

The tunnels' full extent is, even so, still unknown. Many have been cleared of rubbish, so it is possible to see how they have been hewn out of sandstone and finished with mid-Victorian brick vaulting. The size of the largest comes as a wonderful surprise – an area known informally as the Banqueting Hall, it has a six-metre-high ceiling – but even the narrowest sections of tunnel are tall enough for a grown man to walk through without stooping. Another section, still to be excavated, is thought to have been so large that for a while it was used for drilling troops in bad weather.

Over the last twenty years, dozens of hard-working volunteers have managed to clear or part-clear great lengths of tunnel in three distinct areas. Their hope is that in time these will be found to be interconnecting, but no link-tunnels have been discovered so far and the consensus seems to be that it could take as long – if not longer – to clear the labyrinth as it took Williamsons' gangs to dig them out in the first place.

Why Williamson did it is anyone's guess. The most popular theory is that his motives were purely philanthropic and that, as rich men sometimes do, he found work and wages for men in need of both. There are well-known examples of this, and several from Williamson's own time, but few job creation schemes lasted as long as this one seems to have done, which could be one of the reasons why another, somewhat more exotic theory refuses to go away.

From the start, Williamson remained highly secretive about his plans, refusing at every turn to discuss how many men he employed and why. This left a void and from somewhere came the idea that he belonged to a bizarre religious group. In the expectation of some kind of imminent apocalypse, the group was said to be planning some kind of underground redoubt, maybe even a whole subterranean city along the lines envisaged by H. G. Wells in *War of the Worlds*.

Here again there is no documentation to support the idea, but Williamson is known to have been a religious man. During his lifetime, Liverpool is similarly known to have had several millennial cults of one sort or another, membership of which might explain why the tunnels' creator was unwilling to discuss them and why he never, ever invited anyone to take a look around.

Happily, their modern custodians have no such

qualms. The labyrinth, or at least portions of it, is open to the public, although even an extended visit is unlikely to dispel the mystery of its genesis.

Woodstock Palace

Oxfordshire

EVERYONE KNOWS BLENHEIM PALACE near Woodstock, but the loss of Woodstock Palace near Blenheim means that for most visitors the name doesn't ring even the tiniest bell.

In a sense all we have now of the former royal palace is the Treaty of Woodstock. It was signed here in 1247 and under its terms the mournfully named Llewelyn the Last (1223–82) handed much of Wales over to Henry III as a prelude to its eventual conquest by Henry's son, Edward I.

Of the building itself, nothing remains, although since 1961 a carved stone plinth has marked its position across the wide valley from Sir John Vanbrugh's great baroque masterpiece. Its total disappearance is remarkable because by the standards of medieval England, it was a singularly large and remarkable place, and one with a very long history. There is no evidence for the legend that Alfred the Great had his court on the site, but the Saxon High Council or Witan certainly met at Woodstock, and following the Norman invasion it became a favourite royal retreat at the centre of a huge hunting ground.

By 1129, more than seven miles of Cotswold-stone wall

had been built around the estate on the orders of Henry I, creating what was in effect the country's first safari park or zoo. The king kept his lions and camels at Woodstock, possibly even tigers, although presumably not all of them roamed free. He also had England's first porcupine, such exotic species being popular gifts for noblemen and princes to give each other during visits.

Everyone living in the area had already been ordered out, mostly to the village of Old Woodstock, enabling the wall builders to salvage any useful material from the abandoned cottages. Two decades later, this process accelerated after Henry II announced his intention to build a palace on the site of his grandfather's old hunting lodge.

This meant moving the animals out like the villagers before them (many of them to the royal menagerie at the Tower of London, and gradually a much grander building began to take shape. Henry had been explicit about wanting the largest palace in Europe, which it never was, although it included several spacious courtyards, an impressive gatehouse and no fewer than six individual chapels. The project also included the creation of a second village, New Woodstock, to accommodate the people needed to service such a large establishment and the retinues of visiting guests.

Thereafter, the king spent a good deal of time at Woodstock, and indeed had his first row here with the 'turbulent priest' Thomas Becket in 1163. The palace was also the birthplace of the Black Prince, where his sister Mary married the powerful Duke of Brittany, and where the future Elizabeth I was imprisoned for almost a year by her Catholic sibling Mary. As this indicates, Woodstock had fallen slightly out of favour once the Tudors supplanted the Plantagenets. Henry VII commissioned some new building work, and Henry VIII went there to hunt. But Elizabeth spent her time in a lodge in the park because, when described by a visitor in 1551, the palace had 'for many years past ... decayed'.

Much later, James I visited often, but despite having a set of rooms restored he preferred to sleep in a tent. Clearly Woodstock's time as a royal palace was drawing to a close, and the final chapters played out against the background of a civil war. Briefly used to house soldiers loyal to Charles I, it was overrun by parliamentary troops in 1646, sealing its fate.

Badly damaged, no attempt was made at restoration and just as the peasants' cottages had been quarried under Cromwell, the palace's ancient fabric began to be sold off to the highest bidder. The Roundheads generally weren't great hunters either, and with the park degenerating as fast as the buildings, any visits to Woodstock made by king and court after the Restoration seem to have been short and unmemorable.

By 1704 it was all over. Rewarding John Churchill with a dukedom for his decisive victory at the Battle of Blenheim, Queen Anne saw the rundown estate as the perfect gift for her finest soldier. Churchill was accordingly granted the Manor of Woodstock, together with the immense sums of money needed to build and furnish somewhere appropriate to his new status as Duke of Marlborough.

The old palace became a temporary home to the architect, and indeed a marked cooling of Vanbrugh's relationship with Duchess Sarah Churchill is sometimes given as the reason for its final demolition. But in truth Sarah fell out with everyone eventually, even her best friend the queen, and while she may not have liked the idea of Vanbrugh as a neighbour, it's equally likely that no one wanted a mouldering semi-ruin spoiling the view from Blenheim. In 1720, Woodstock was razed and every last brick and plank carted away.

Woolworths

HIGH-STREET NAMES COME AND GO ALL THE TIME, but until its disappearance in 2009, Woolworths *was* the high street and had been for almost a hundred years.

The name is still used online, but the loss of more than 800 high street stores and 27,000 jobs made Woolworths one of the highest-profile casualties of the global recession. Trading as F. W. Woolworth & Co., the company had opened its first store in Liverpool in 1909, long enough ago for British shoppers to have forgotten (if indeed they ever knew) that Frank Winfield Woolworth was an American and had begun with a chain of 'five-and-dimes' in the USA.

To millions of customers, 'Woolies' still seems as English as a cup of tea, and from the start its decision to offer so many goods at just 3d or 6d (1.5p and 2.5p) meant that the first store was an immediate success. In less than five years there were more than forty of them, and ten times that number by the end of the following decade. The company reached its peak in the 1960s, by which time there were well over 1,100 branches, giving it a presence in virtually every town and city.

For much of its history the stores' great strength was that they sold so many different products, and not just clothes, toys, electrical goods and confectionary. Though arguably most famous for its pick-and-mix sweets, Woolworths had something for nearly everyone, and for a long time it could genuinely be said that almost every family shopped there.

Unfortunately, success can breed complacency, and although new management tried new things, Woolworths gradually fell behind its competitors. The major supermarkets evolved to begin taking bites out of Woolworths, and some of its traditional markets – for example, recorded music – simply disappeared. Many branches were also too large (some as large as department stores) and when the move to out-of-town locations really began to damage high-street sales, the company was too slow to move. More than a few branches were effectively left stranded in areas that had been abandoned by many of its core customers.

Different attempts were made to change with the times, such as offering a click-and-collect service to challenge Internet retailers such as Amazon and the Big Red Book as a sort of Argos catalogue rival. But at best this was too little too late, and after rejecting a buyout offer that valued the chain at just £50 million, Woolworths appeared to be on its last legs.

When it finally crashed, everyone was shocked. On high streets around Britain, people expressed their fondness for Woolworths, but falling revenues told their own story: people were fond of it but didn't shop at Woolworths any more, and hadn't for years. A rush of nostalgia meant there were enormous queues outside many of the stores towards the end – just as there had been in Liverpool ninety-nine years earlier – and on one day the tills rang to the sound of £27 million, an all-time record for the group.

Woolworths was, nevertheless, a goner. Several potential buyers had come forward, one offering to buy it for £1 until this was blocked by the firm's bankers. But with debts of around £385 million, no one was interested in reviving the Woolworths Britons had come to know and love. Just months shy of its centenary, one of the most famous names on the high street finally ran out of steam.

Wrecking

Devon

MARINE SALVAGE HAS BECOME A SOPHISTICATED global business worth many tens of billions of dollars annually, but for centuries coastal communities took it upon themselves to liberate goods and materials from ships that had come to grief in the shallows.

The activity was called wrecking and, particularly in parts of Devon and Cornwall, profits from it could make a significant contribution to the lives of those involved. So significant, in fact, that under the terms of an eighteenth-century law it was specifically forbidden for anyone to display a light on the shore in such a way as to lure a likely-looking vessel onto the rocks.

From the sixteenth century onwards, wreckers were active elsewhere too, for example in the Pentland Firth and on the treacherous sands around the Thames Estuary. The south-west was a particularly good hunting ground, however, because ships taking advantage of the Gulf Stream would often pass very close to land, more than occasionally with disastrous results. Over the years, many thousands of ships were lost in this way, holding out the possibility of a good living for anyone willing to risk the law and his life[20] by stealing anything of value.

There is no case on record of a ship being intentionally enticed onto the rocks by such people, but examples of locals rescuing shipwrecked crew members were also woefully thin on the ground until 1870. After this it became possible to offer rewards for such a service and individuals known as Receivers of Wreck were increasingly employed to control these potentially inflammatory situations.

Typically this was done by offering cash payments to civilians assisting shipwrecked sailors, where previously they might have attempted to pillage the ship. The law also allowed for the Receiver to be armed, possibly even to 'hurt, maim or kill' anyone acting unlawfully, although his chief focus was to identify the owner of the stricken cargo, to prevent anything being looted, and eventually to ensure that the two were reunited.

At one time employed by the Board of Trade and later Customs & Excise, the Receiver of Wreck eventually came under the control of the Maritime and Coastguard Agency. As the threat from wreckers gradually died down, his legal power to kill was curtailed (according to some sources only in 1995, but the office is still responsible for safeguarding the rights of owners, while recognizing the crucial role a licensed marine-salvage professional can play.

Just occasionally, however, we are treated to a reminder of how things used to be, most recently in 2007 when the MSC *Napoli* was hit by a ferocious storm. Damaged, abandoned and drifting off the Cornish coast, the container ship was eventually taken in tow and then beached near Sidmouth on the world-famous Jurassic Coast.

---

20. Wreckers were not only at risk from drowning but were occasionally hanged for theft.

Besides dumping oil and hazardous chemicals in this environmentally important area, the *Napoli* had lost between 100 and 200 of its large shipping containers. As these drifted towards the shore, an almost eighteenth-century scene unfolded as scavenging locals made their way down to the beach to see what they could find. Despite an official warning from the Receiver of Wreck for them to stay away, wine casks, make-up, motorcar components and an estimated fifty German motorbikes rapidly disappeared.

Behind them, these modern-day wreckers left a scene of unimaginable squalor, with unwanted goods ripped from their packaging, broken and left lying in the filth of an already polluted beauty spot. It was a rude awakening for anyone with a nostalgic yearning for the old ways of doing things, and a reminder that the traditional ways are not always the best. The habit of wrecking may be lost, but that's no bad thing.

PICTURE CREDITS

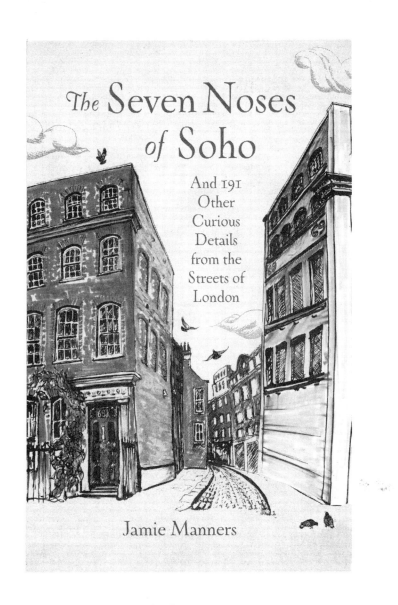

The Seven Noses of Soho
978-1-78243-461-0
£12.99 hardback

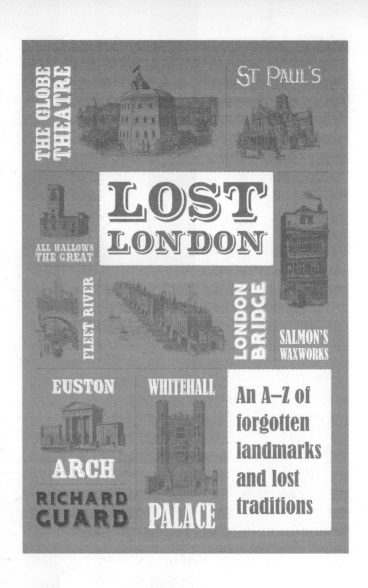

Lost London
978-1-78243-333-0
£7.99 paperback